THINK SMART
WORK SMART
THE DEFINITIVE STUDENT GUIDE
TO LESS IS MORE!

MAX YOUR DEGREE

THINK SMART
WORK SMART

THE DEFINITIVE STUDENT GUIDE
TO LESS IS MORE!

Part I
of the

MAX YOUR DEGREE

Series

By
Michael O'Grady
Principal Lecturer in Digital Media
The University of Huddersfield, UK

PLANET-STUDENT
www.planet-student.com

MAX YOUR DEGREE

© Copyright 2017   Michael O'Grady

Published by   Planet Student
                www.planet-student.com

All rights reserved.
No part of this publication may be reproduced, stored in a retrieval system or transmitted in any form or by any means, electronic, mechanical, photocopying, recording, scanning or otherwise, except under the terms of the Copyright, Designs and Patents act 1988 or under the terms of a licence issued by the Copyright Licensing Agency Limited, Barnard's Inn, 86 Fetter Lane, London, EC4 1EN, UK, without the permission in writing of the Publisher. Requests to the Publisher should be addressed to Planet Student, by emailing admin@planet-student.com.

Designations used by companies to distinguish their products are often claimed as trademarks. All brand names and product names used in this book are trade names, service marks, trademarks or registered trademarks of their respective owners. The publisher is not associated with any product or vendor mentioned in this book.

This publication is designed to provide accurate and authoritative information in regard to the subject matter covered. It is sold on the understanding that the publisher is not engaged in rendering professional services. If professional advice or other expert assistance is required the services of a competent professional should be sought.

Michael O'Grady has asserted his right under the Copyright, Designs and Patents Act, 1988 to be identified as the author of this work.

A catalogue record for this book is available from the British Library

ISBN-13 **978-0-9935289-0-3**

Cover Illustration: Graham Watts
Design: Graham Watts
Layout: Angela Lin

ACKNOWLEDGEMENTS

TO MY WONDERFUL WIFE WHO NURTURES AND GUIDES ME WITH TENDERNESS AND WISDOM. SHE HAS BEEN AN ESSENTIAL MOTIVATOR AND EDITOR IN MY JOURNEY TO BECOME A PUBLISHED AUTHOR.

MAX YOUR DEGREE

CONTENTS

Preface	**Welcome**	ix
Chapter 1	**Introduction**	1
Chapter 2	**Time as Currency**	15
Chapter 3	**Good Timing**	27
Chapter 4	**Personal Values**	37
Chapter 5	**Goal Setting**	47
Chapter 6	**Getting Started**	61
Chapter 7	**Habits Worth Developing**	77
Chapter 8	**How To Fail Your Degree**	103
Chapter 9	**Technology**	111
Chapter 10	**Summary**	141
Chapter 11	**References & Influences**	149

MAX YOUR DEGREE

PREFACE
WELCOME

"Love the life you live. Live the life you love."
— Bob Marley

If you are considering studying for an undergraduate degree, or have actually begun the process, this book is for you. Whether you want to aim for a First, exceed your natural abilities, have more time for fun or to just focus on a career direction; this book is for you. If you have been at university for a while already and are struggling with morale or feeling unfulfilled, this book is also for you. It's a book for any student, on any year, on any course.

Even though you may be about to complete your final year, there are still lots of time- and money-saving tips that will support you beyond graduation. Maybe you already know the answers and feel that this book is not for you. It might then be for your parents, who can refer to it at times when you may need a gentle reminder!

I've spent over 75% of my adult life in Higher Education, providing me with a wealth of experience both as a student and as a lecturer. Having studied for a BSc, MSc and PhD, I have lived seven years as a student and nineteen as a lecturer.

During this time I've been fortunate enough to see both sides of the academic fence, giving and receiving in equal measure — support, wisdom and inspiration. For me, the most cherished aspect of teaching has always been the amazing relationships that I have been privileged to have shared with my students. This may have been in the lecture setting or in a more pastoral context, dealing with life issues and personal problems.

*"People think my life has been tough,
but I think it has been a wonderful journey.
The older you get, the more you realize,
it's not what happens, but how you deal with it."*
— Tina Turner

My initial career, as a consulting civil engineer, allowed me to travel the globe and provided opportunities for developing invaluable insights into the world of commerce and industry. I learnt at an early stage, that having a degree in itself is often insufficient in securing the job of ones' dreams. Life skills, self-development, organisational and personal abilities are all equally important in securing prime positions, particularly in an increasingly competitive world. As a father of two adult children who are now well on their way to forging their own careers, I understand the anxieties and uncertainties that you yourself may be facing.

Hopefully this book will provide you with the answers to questions that I have discovered through numerous (and often painful) mistakes that I have made along my own journey, without the anguish of having to experience them yourself!

This is a book to help you with academic study. Whilst I'm an academic myself, I decided early on to appeal to as wide an audience as possible; strict grammar and stuffy language would likely turn you off to the well-intentioned messages. So I've deliberately made the voice informal and approachable; that of a family friend who wants you to have the best advice. It's no accident that I've concatenated words. Just make sure you don't do the same with your formal academic writing!

What was my motivation for writing this book?

Whilst there is a plethora of study-based books available, there is little in the way of comprehensive guides providing undergraduates with support during the transition into higher education and beyond. This is often a time when we are already encountering challenges relating to identity, independence, role and relationships as we move from adolescence to adulthood. In the academic sense, we are expected to shift from (relatively) dependent learning to being self-sufficient problem solvers.

"The only impossible journey is the one you don't begin."
— Anthony Robbins

There is an increasing drive from policy makers, institutions and industry to increase the creativity, inventiveness, enterprise and social skills of the half a million people entering UK universities every year... but how? This book makes a bold step to prepare you for these challenges, to make you smarter, more decisive, more productive; ultimately allowing you to lead a more vital life.

I also wanted to learn how to self-publish so that I could pass on the learning to my students. Solving the problem of something to write about quickly turned in to a 125,000 word (and counting) thesis and so I had to break it down into bite-sized chunks. You are at the beginning of that very first chunk; Book 1. There are more to come.

It's always immensely uplifting to see students graduating; for some the journey will have been a breeze, for others an immense struggle. For the rest, somewhere in between. Often, students only need to have someone believe in them in order to sustain the effort needed to succeed. I hope that this book will provide you with the insights, strategies and encouragement to help you succeed on this fabulous journey.

One of the biggest challenges in writing this series of books has been overcoming my own insecurities, limiting beliefs and anxiety of peer review. Universities are a melting-pot of some of the best minds in society; not only the lecturers, but the student body too. In publishing, I am holding myself up to your collective gaze and critical comment, so I hope my effort is of real value to you.

Please feel free to email me or leave comments on the **maxyourdegree.com** website. I really do care and want to hear your feedback.

My lovely wife really deserves more praise than she will allow me to write here. I have benefited greatly from her patience, encouragement and her editing of mistakes and misconceptions in my initial drafts. Only I know how lucky we are to have had her input.

My students continue to be a great influence and driving force for me. Many thanks to them and the ones who follow. I wish you all well at university and hope that you are able to have the immense fun and learning that you deserve, discovering along the way that you can get exactly what you want from life as long as you are smart about it.

This book is all about getting more from your time at university, to help you on your exciting journey. Now read on...

MAX YOUR DEGREE

CHAPTER 1
INTRODUCTION

*"If you focus on results, you will never change.
If you focus on change, you will get results."*
— Jack Dixon.

An undergraduate degree is a phenomenal three or four year experience, where the typical student has access to great freedoms and is subject to (relatively) few demands and pressures. You will have increased social contact and meet lots of new people, with some of them becoming life-long friends.

You may be living away from home for the first time, joining clubs, travelling, socialising and doing a whole host of new things. It's a period of great personal expansion, pushing back boundaries and accelerating personal growth. You will likely never do so much in such a condensed period again. It can be thrilling and frightening at the same time; welcome to student life.

I believe that your undergraduate days are truly the best years of your life. If you are not enjoying university life then this book will hopefully provide you with a starting point from which you can work through your issues.

Lots of different things come up for people as they engage in personal growth activities. You will possibly come across some obstacles whilst reading and working through some of the exercises. Don't worry about it, be gentle with yourself and try as much as possible to reflect on what is happening in your life.

This book can make a dramatic difference to you, whatever your reason for picking it up. It deals with:

- *how you approach your studies*
- *the results you can achieve*
- *how much fun and free-time you could enjoy and*
- *your ambitions for what you want to do with your degree.*

I have three really focused messages I want you to understand, based on decades working both sides of the university divide; as a student and lecturer. They are:

- *you need to **differentiate** yourself from those around you*
- *you need to optimise your efforts by working **smart** and*
- *your university years are at least as much about your **personal growth** as about the course content.*

Differentiate. There will be potentially hundreds (thousands?) of similarly qualified graduates leaving university the same time as you, all vying for the same graduate positions. By differentiating yourself from your peers and those on similar courses at other universities, you make it easier for your dream employer to see and employ you.

How you view the world; how you deal with the ups and downs; how you aspire and become ambitious; and how you become certain of your future all show in the way you present yourself at interview. The greater your involvement with your future and its plans, the greater your differentiation and the more convincing you will be to others.

Smart. Anyone can work hard, but there are only 24 hours in a day, no matter who you are! So the amount of real and useful work you can do in a day is controlled less by the hours and more by the direction, application and appropriateness of the effort. Seven hours working smart beats seven hours working hard, any day.

There are so many ways of working smart and we look at many in this book, some new and challenging. You may therefore need to amend your approach or behaviours to be smarter. Easier said than done, but we look at that too.

Personal Growth. I tell my students that no more than 49% of university is about the degree course content. At least 51% is about the soft skills and personal growth.

Students constantly underestimate the value employers put on: tenacity, consistency, positive thinking, team-working, social skills, problem solving, time management and many other attributes commensurate with the world of professional work.

Personal growth might be the area that requires most development and provide the biggest challenges to you, but there are chapters in the book that will begin to tease out the best in you and let you see your part in your future.

When I was an undergraduate, I thought I had all the time in the world and it's only now in later life, that I realise how much more I could have achieved with the right mental attitude and appropriate strategies at my fingertips. The motivator for me to write this book is to provide you with a glimpse into your vast potential. I hope to give you the knowledge and some of the tools to help you achieve an ambitious future.

"If your emotional abilities aren't in hand, if you don't have self-awareness, if you are not able to manage your distressing emotions, if you can't have empathy and have effective relationships, then no matter how smart you are, you are not going to get very far."
— *Daniel Goleman*

If you liken your degree to a long car journey from the UK, perhaps crossing through Europe, Russia and on to China, you would ensure that your vehicle was extremely well serviced and you would probably take many spares to get you through the arduous journey. Likewise, preparation and awareness of the degree journey is invaluable.

For many undergraduates, there is little preparation for what is to come. Freshers may not always have an understanding of how intense the academic challenge will be and may never have experienced the effect that advanced knowledge and new experiences have on aspirations and ambitions whilst at university.

By reading this book, taking its messages seriously, working on the exercises and practicing the lessons learnt, you have the chance to change your life forever and become a super-focused student.

There's a lot of preparatory work involved — changes in your expectations, changes in the way you approach problems and the way you use your time.

"SEVEN HOURS WORKING SMART, BEATS SEVEN HOURS WORKING HARD..."

Did you know that you have a range of different Values in your life relating to family, relationships, work and more? Knowing what they are and tailoring your life's purpose in harmony with your Values is a major factor in being happy. Many people are unhappy, doing things against core Values they weren't even aware they held. We will be looking at your Life Values later in the book.

As the old saying goes, "Nothing can be said to be certain except death and taxes". However, I believe there is a third certainty and, whilst life is inherently not fair, everyone is faced with lots of opportunities during each and every day. So a slight modification is... *Only three things in life are certain: death, taxes and opportunities.*

"Serendipity always rewards the prepared."
— *Katori Hall*

This book is all about making you aware and opening your mind to the myriad of opportunities that lie along your chosen path and which, if followed, are going to provide you with amazing results and advances along the road that is your future. I mention many times in this book ways in which you can differentiate yourself from other students and graduates. In fact, if you are to find a great job, you need to stand head and shoulders above your competition.

One way in which this book differentiates itself from others on the subject is to deal with things that are not seemingly related to your degree study... but arguably, infinitely more important than it. This book deals with **you**.

I'm going to show you a way forward, not only to be the most fabulous and brilliant student you can be, but better; how to start visualising your future, how to get serious about getting where you want to go and how you can develop into being the person you want to be.

If you haven't thought about who you want to be or what you want to do yet, then you are one among many. Now is the perfect time to reflect on what you do want in life. Only you know what you want and you may not even know that much yet.

Reading this book and doing the exercises with commitment and focus will help you plan your life. It will be a fabulous journey and I'm incredibly proud to be playing a part in it.

To reiterate an earlier point, there are always opportunities. If your mind is closed to *see things differently, hear other opinions* or *believe in different outcomes*... then you are shutting yourself off from opportunity.

If you follow this guidance with any form of commitment, you will find opportunities open up to you, or rather, the opportunities that are constantly presenting themselves suddenly become visible. Whether you take these opportunities or not is up to you.

By taking such actions and allowing your behaviours to change, you will not only open up your life considerably, you will get a better class of degree. You will also be more successful at what you aim for and you will get more enjoyment out of your life. Big claims, but... following your life's purpose is perhaps the most fulfilling thing you can do. So I'm going to help you determine what your purpose is and present the tools to help get you there.

"ONLY THREE THINGS ARE CERTAIN IN LIFE: DEATH, TAXES AND OPPORTUNITY."

The average student works hard and this is a requirement for attaining an honours degree, but many struggle to do things as well as they would like. They continually come up against their own resistance at working or changing, they do things twice, three times. They waste time by being inefficient and not concentrating. They can waste time literally for the purpose of wasting time. Watching TV, social networking, playing computer games, getting up late on a class day, missing lectures, and drinking to excess are pretty good examples.

This book is about making you into a **smart** student, not necessarily a hard worker, though the combination of working smart and hard is unbeatable. Smart students know when to work hard and when to work intelligently.

Working smart has several advantages. Doing exactly what is required gives you top marks and doing your work in the least amount of time gives you a chance to follow your interests and have lots of fun.

I've been a hard worker all my life, my strong work ethic is something I am very proud of. I can even persuade myself I am being lazy if I take the occasional hour off to watch television or to chill. But working hard can be very draining and one of the lessons that I have had to learn is that hard-working people need to work hard at taking time off.

You've probably heard the expression "work hard, play hard". This is really good advice because you need a work-life balance. So if you don't want to work hard at your studies, you need to start thinking and working smarter. If you want to stand out above all your peers, then working smart and hard will get you there.

"Promise me you'll always remember: You're braver than you believe, and stronger than you seem, and smarter than you think."
— A. A. Milne

This book makes the assumption that, whether you are working hard to attain a place at university; are already in first year; or even passed an academic year or two, there are still quantum leaps you can make in terms of achievements and goals being met, as well as with your own satisfaction, happiness and fun.

You may however have limiting beliefs that slow you down or stop you taking opportunities that might otherwise work out for you. Perhaps you are overly negative or lacking in confidence or perhaps you just don't see what your future looks like. You might be the opposite; utterly confident in the future... whatever it works out to be. Either way, taking a long, hard look at yourself is a worthy exercise. One which we will cover shortly.

As already mentioned there are only 24 hours in the day. You might be someone who willingly wastes time, you might even wish your life away. Have you ever heard someone say "I wish it was Friday?" If they say that on a Monday, and they were to get their wish granted, then 5/7 (or 71%) of their week would disappear. That's great if you like continual weekends, but the implication is that instead of living to say 85 years, you would only live 29% of that age: 25 years.

So don't wish your life away and instead analyse why you might want time to go faster. It's probably because you're not getting out of it what you should. Once you know how to value your time properly, everything else starts to come into focus.

All these things are discussed in the book. Take it one chapter at a time and see how positively it can affect your life.

HOW TO GET THE MOST FROM THIS BOOK

I recommend that you be more than just a passive reader. To get the best out of the book's many messages, I suggest that you engage fully with the exercises. The words you read here are not a magic pill to change your life forever; rather, they provide the framework of strategies and thought-provoking questions for you to start to figure out your very personal path in life.

There are therefore numerous exercises and downloadable worksheets on the **www.maxyourdegree.com** website that you are strongly encouraged to engage in. It is only by opening your mind to new ideas and different ways of working that you achieve a step-change to the results you deserve. The more you engage with these new ways of thinking, the more relevant their routes and answers will be to you.

Lots of new ideas and opportunities are presented in the book and it is important that you don't rush over each chapter. Read slowly, mull over the concepts, try to mesh these new ideas with your own experiences and try to imagine modifying your approach to life with the new information presented.

Is xxxx idea worth trying? What could you get out of it? What could it mean to you if it worked? What would you think of yourself if it did? Is it worth making the effort?

I suggest that you take the contents of this book to heart, make it a very personal learning journey. However, like most things in life (riding a bike, using Facebook or cooking), we learn much better by *doing*. Experiential learning... learning from experience. It's the ultimate way of making the knowledge stick and for it to have a positive effect on us.

So I recommend doing the exercises in the book as they come along. There are several and some may take you several hours or several days, especially if you are trying to decide and reflect on the life-changing ideas presented:

- **Chapter 2 and 3** show a different approach to how you might see and value time

- **Chapter 4** encourages you to think about and complete the Life Values Statement form. Do you know your Life Values?

- **Chapter 5** encourages you to think of and write out your short-, medium- and long-term goals. What do you want to achieve?

- **Chapter 6** presents you with a blank template for you to write in your daily / weekly schedule in-hourly slots. Write it down, get it done!

- **Chapter 7** looks at developing some good habits and behaviours across a range of subjects including strengthening your emotional resilience
- **Chapter 8** takes a reverse psychology and tongue-in-cheek route to improving the view of your studies by showing you how to fail your degree
- **Chapter 9** reviews much of the general and specific technology available to you to make your studies easier and your learning more efficient and enjoyable.

"..IT'S ALL ABOUT HOW YOU DEAL WITH CURRENT SITUATUONS THAT MATTERS. YOU ARE NOT YOUR PAST"

It's easy to read on and not do the work, however, this is about moving your life forward and becoming a **smarter** student, one who differentiates themselves at every turn. It's better to experience these life-changing behaviours rather than merely reading about them. Only with practice do they become part of your new way of working.

As you read, I suggest that you make notes in a notebook about each chapter. These can include ideas, reinforcement of concepts, action plans and questions. It's usually when we are least stressed that we have our best ideas, so it's a good idea to keep a notebook and pen by your bed.

Don't worry about making notes in this book or highlighting sections; it's your book... your life. Take time out to reflect on the concepts and questions it raises.

Have a goal (or two) in mind as you read. This can be very beneficial in helping you slot the new information in to your existing framework of approaching and doing things. Here are a few over-arching goals you might consider for your degree years:

- *I want a First Class Honours degree*
- *I want a better degree than my current results indicate*
- *I want a good degree and to have more fun in the process*
- *I want to be top of the class*
- *I want my dream job*
- *I want to find out what it is that I want in life.*

This book is all about providing you with choices in life. The more information you have about your opportunities and the more experience you have, then the better your focus on what you want to do and the more chances you have of achieving your aims.

The sad truth for many people is that they blame others for their situation and future; but it's all down to the individual. Welcome to your future... where you are in the driving seat.

"A smart man makes a mistake, learns from it, and never makes that mistake again. But a wise man finds a smart man and learns from him how to avoid the mistake altogether."
— *Roy H. Williams*

I have used a great many quotes in this book. I've had great fun in choosing them and I hope you take inspiration from their crystallised wisdom.

So let's get started by looking at your working day a little differently. I want you to be more enthusiastic in directing your valuable time at those things that need doing so that you have more time to do the things you want to do. So, the next chapter looks at those very important issues of time, money and your degree. Time to start putting it all in to perspective.

MAX YOUR DEGREE

CHAPTER 2
TIME AS CURRENCY

"Lost time is never found again."
— Benjamin Franklin

Most of us undervalue our time. We waste it, quite literally. People will even do menial jobs just to avoid doing things they should do. When I have a sudden burst of activity, my wife will want to know which of my important tasks I am avoiding (she is invariably correct in this assumption).

In the same situation, the typical student will reply to email the instant it is received. Twitter and Facebook messaging become a welcome break to the continuous need for study or revision. Chilling with friends, a spontaneous night out for a drink... lots of different ways of using time up when there is plenty of work to be done.

How many times in a day or week do you zone-out of your current task, staring in to space, thinking about something that happened in the past or something that could happen in the future? You might be socialising with friends, travelling on the bus or train... or worse... doing it while studying.

There are only so many hours until the next assignment is handed in or until the next exam is scheduled. So you need to make the most of each 24 hours and I'm not asking you to rob hours from your sleep. You will see via this process that you have more than enough hours for study in each day and, when done correctly, a lot more time to socialise and have fun.

2.1 The Value of a Degree

"The roots of education are bitter, but the fruit is sweet."
— Aristotle

There's no doubt that the current way in which UK student fees and maintenance grants are administered, graduates exit with (and sometimes without) a degree and several tens of £000s of debt. So what makes it a worthwhile proposition in the first place?

There are several reasons why undergraduate study is beneficial, including broadening of the mind, meeting life-long friends you would never have otherwise have met, an opening up of career paths and greatly enhanced career opportunities with salaries to match.

Some jobs just aren't available to you without a degree. Medicine and veterinary surgeons require at least a Bachelor's degree and further study to be allowed to practice. Degree study prepares you for problem solving and researching, whilst enhancing your people-skills and project management abilities. It is also the perfect start to settle down to life-long learning, something many companies and most industry bodies want from their members.

So, graduates have a head-start on the corporate ladder and most companies have a career progression structure where each level has a pay band associated with it. It is expected that graduates will progress up this structure as they gain experience, take on responsibilities and demonstrate profit- or value-increasing activities for their company.

All of the above tend to, on average, put a graduate's pay and benefits above that of hourly paid staff. Of course, the latter clock on and off at set times, are free to spend the remainder of the day at leisure without worrying about tasks they didn't complete whilst at work.

Graduates however tend to have jobs where a minimum amount of work and deliverables are expected, irrespective of the hours worked, but with greater flexibility of working. This typically manifests itself as an increase in weekly hours and the likelihood for many of having to bring work home.

Different studies broadly agree that graduate pay is greater than non-graduates with starting salaries typically 50% greater with a degree, compared to non-degree people. The Higher Education Statistics Agency (HESA, www.hesa.ac.uk) figures for 2013/14 show that the average graduate starting salary across all disciplines and regions was approximately £22,000 whilst equivalent non-graduate salaries were around £15,300.

For a typical case then, graduates earn more, year in, year out. Several newspapers create shock headlines that the difference in a life-time can be as much as £500,000, though there is broad agreement that the lifetime differential is somewhere between £100k and £500k.

Calculations are a little uncertain as we look at retirement age. Retired graduates are generally at the higher end of their earning capabilities and for someone on £70,000 pa, the 10 years difference between retiring at 55 versus 65 could be close to £700k. Conversely, a bricklayer will be on their life-maximum pay during their youth and early middle-age resulting from a combination of physical fitness, fluency of skills and any building boom that may or may not occur. Pay for manual work tends not to increase in older age due to reducing fitness.

Let's look at the mechanics of a simple example of two 21 year olds, Person **A** being a graduate starting on £22,000 pa and Person **B** a non-graduate on £15,300. Let's assume that with inflation, natural pay rises and promotions, the yearly pay of each increases by 3% (clearly a gross simplification).

When they both reach 65, the graduate will be on £77k pa and the non-graduate on £56k pa. Adding up every year's pay for each, the total life-time earnings are £1.95M and £1.4M respectively, a difference of slightly over £500k. Of course there are extremes, there are some very famous millionaire non-graduates (Alan Sugar springs to mind) and many graduates can be found filling shelves at a local supermarket. However, averaged out among the current 1.7million UK undergraduates each year, these statistics are a good indication of the value of a great education, (Search: *hesa general student numbers*).

This puts in to perspective your student debt, which while averaging out at £44,000 (Search: *sutton trust degrees of debt*), is held by the UK Government and you only pay it back in monthly increments, assuming your salary exceeds £21,000 pa. If you are on Plan 2 (i.e. you started your loan finance after 1st September 2012) and earning £25,000 pa, your monthly payment is only £30, probably less than either your mobile rental or broadband package.

2.2 The Value of Time

"Time is money."
— Benjamin Franklin

A great way for you to value time is to literally apply a monetary sum to your working hours. The UK has a National Minimum Wage, currently £7.05 per hour for 21 to 24 year olds, (£5.60 per hour for 18 to 20 year olds). If you are 18 to 20 and serving fries at a fast-food restaurant you will be paid a minimum of £5.60 for each and every hour that you are clocked-in. Recently upgraded, the new UK Living Wage is slightly more at £8.45 per hour for those 25 and older, (£9.75 per hour in London) with accredited companies.

In fact, you could spend the rest of your active life working on hourly rates... and many people around the world do. Many have no choice and some even opt for that lifestyle. However, your degree is costing you quite a lot of money. I don't need to remind you of the study and accommodation fees, travel and socialising... it's all building up.

The problem is, if you project your life forward as a minimum wage worker after graduation, you will find it hard to repay much of your debt. With a degree, your equivalent hourly rate will be much greater, so I want to get you thinking about valuing your time differently. I want you to consider every hour that goes by as being worth something more meaningful; a much higher value than the preceding figures. This way, you'll be less likely to waste your time.

For the majority of people with a positive income (living off their earnings) rather than students who live off borrowings, the hourly-value formula is quite easy. You take the number of hours that can be worked in a year and divide it into the annual wage or salary. If we assume the average worker has four weeks holiday per year plus an extra week for Bank Holidays and works a 37.5 hour week, this amounts to 1762.5 hours in the working year or (52-4-1) x 37.5 = 47 x 37.5.

For a salary of £30,000, this equates to £17 per hour. I am of course ignoring the fact that salaried staff get paid for Bank Holidays and for their annual holidays as well, so this rate is even lower (1950 hours giving £15.40 per hour).

As a student, you are in a situation similar to an entrepreneur — your future reward is directly related to your effort. This doesn't always happen in salaried employment, but what it means is that we cannot assume that every hour spent working is productive. We cannot guarantee that each hour of study is spent with 100% concentration and so we have to modify the productive hours by applying a correction factor.

It is considered generous by entrepreneurs to factor in a value of 3.0, though it is more likely to be 4.0. So that in an 8 hour working day and using a factor of 4, only 2 hours are truly productive and provide a direct path to remuneration. So that's 8hrs / 4.0 = 2hrs.

What this means in reality is that you need to multiply your hourly rate by this factor. Your hourly rate is therefore far greater than first calculated.

Using the previously calculated figure of £17/hr and a correction factor of 4, we get to £68/hr (£17/hr x 4 = £68/hr). Now you might not agree with the correction factor, but just be honest with yourself; how often does an hour of study actually equate to one full concentrated hour? Sure, you will have days when you feel on top of everything and worked harder than ever before. But most days you will likely get distracted by someone passing by, your phone vibrating, email pinging, thoughts of the upcoming party this weekend, by the argument you had with your boyfriend / girlfriend / parents last night or spend time worrying about upcoming assignments or exams.

> "..AS A STUDENT,
> YOU ARE IN A SITUATION SIMILAR
> TO AN ENTREPRENEUR
> – YOUR REWARD IS DIRECTLY
> RELATED TO YOUR EFFORT."

There are lots of things to distract you from the purity of study, and once your mind has been distracted, you can lose concentration for quite a few minutes, then waste more time re-finding your train of thought. The main issue here is to be as realistic and honest as possible to get the hourly value as high as possible and to make the point that **time is important**.

So let's see how this applies to students. You have debt - lots of money going out for a variety of purposes. You may have money coming in through hourly paid or casual labour and some savings from a summer job plus any loans.

Let's put some figures to it. The formula is typically as follows:

$$\text{Hourly rate} = \frac{\text{Factor} \times \text{Money value (£)}}{\text{Time (hours)}} = \frac{4 \times (\text{Income-Tuition-Rent-Expenses})}{(\text{study weeks/year} \times 40\text{hrs/wk})}$$

Note that your fees and living expenses are a greater sum than your income, so the result is negative. However, all we are concerned about is the **magnitude** of the money you will owe. Also, you don't physically handle your university fees, they are paid on your behalf by your finance company. However, the debt is building in your name, so it needs to be accounted for. Let's look at an example.

Example – Sarah

Let's look at an imaginary example of Sarah. She is a first year Law student in university. She earns an income of £1,500 throughout the academic year from a paid job. Her outgoings will be something in the order of:

- £9,000 for university tuition fees per academic year
- £4,400 for accommodation fees (varies widely around the UK, assumed private inclusive accommodation at £100/wk) and
- £2,500 for living expenses (food, travel, clothing, study equipment, socialising etc., again, varies widely).

Her outgoings are therefore £15,500 and her income is £1,500, balancing to £14,000 (£15,500 - £1,500) per year.

Even though this value is a negative income (debt), it still works because it represents the balance-sheet of a single year; money in, money out and time spent.

Assuming Sarah has a 40 week academic calendar and studies 40 hours on each of those weeks, she will put in approximately 1600 hours of study. This relates to £9.00/hr, but multiplying by four gives her hourly rate at £36.00/hr (ignore the minus sign). In the previous formula, we get values like this:

$$\text{Hourly rate} = \frac{4 \times (1500 - 9000 - 4400 - 2500)}{40 \times 40} = \frac{4 \times -£14400}{1600\text{hrs}} = -£36/\text{hr}$$

You can plug in the values that relate to your life quite easily. Your university fees may be more, your rent less or your living expenses more and you might put in considerably more hours of study (hopefully you do!). But whatever the values, your hourly rate will be in the region of £30 to £40/hr. This is the value of your study time.

So this is how I recommend you think about your use of time; for every hour that you're playing computer games it is costing you £36. Every hour spent socialising on Facebook and Twitter is costing you £36. Every hour you're watching television is costing you £36. Of course, it's not actually costing you £36, it just that your time is worth £36/hr when applied to your studies.

Have a quick calculation of how many hours you 'waste' in a week... hours that you know you should be studying, but choose not to. Then multiply by £36. Would you like that money as a weekly income? Okay, so just turn those hours in to study time and reap the rewards a little later. It's called **delayed gratification** and is an idea worth pursuing.

I have no problem in admitting in this book how much of a difference this concept changed my life. It's addressed one of the main problems I knew I had with myself, but was reluctant, unwilling, or unable to do anything about, namely wasting time. There's another name for it... **procrastination**. We look at procrastination-busting strategies later on in the book so stick with it and read on.

> "..FOR EVERY HOUR THAT YOU'RE PLAYING COMPUTER GAMES IT IS COSTING YOU £36. EVERY HOUR SPENT SOCIALISING ON FACEBOOK AND TWITTER IS COSTING YOU £36."

So the next time you feel yourself getting busy by answering a lot of emails, making Facebook comments, Tweeting, going out for a drink, whatever... just think to yourself:

'Is this stopping me earning £36/hr on my studies?
Is it a welcome break from working hard or is it procrastination?'

Anything that prompts you to return to your studies is worth it. But *all work and no play makes Jack a dull boy*, so we have to create a good work/life balance.

Before we address your Life Values and Aims, I want to look at one element of your behaviour which may be stopping you from being the super-smart student you want to be. It's about turning up for appointments and being on time... every time.

Whether it is a lecture, tutorial, workshop, exam, the morning train, meeting your friend at the start of a night out... turning up where and when you agreed is much more important than you may currently think.

Extending the age-old adage *'My word is my bond'* people should expect you to be where you said you would be at a certain time... or worse, expect you not to be there.

So let's investigate a world where you actually arrive for meetings, when and where you said you would. Time for a little time management.

CHAPTER 3
GOOD TIMING

"I never could have done what I have done without the habits of punctuality, order, and diligence, without the determination to concentrate myself on one subject at a time."
— Charles Dickens

A lot of your success will come from how well you manage time. Once you value your time, you can begin to value the time of other people and they get an opportunity of becoming more aware of how valuable time is to you.

Have you ever been stood-up by a potential girlfriend or boyfriend? Have you ever waited outside a pub for a friend, alone and embarrassed, who then apologises after turning up 45 minutes late because... they met someone else and went to another pub for a drink first... or they had to cope with an emergency or some reason or other? How do you feel if you arrange a meeting and the person turns up half an hour late? They've just wasted £18 of your time (£36 x 0.5). What if they forgot to turn up at all? What you should be considering is this; how long are you going to give them before you start utilising your time as you want? How long before you activate a Plan B?

3.1 Punctuality

"Punctuality is the soul of business."
— *Thomas Chandler Haliburton*

The punctuality of someone is a massively strong indicator as to how reliable they are overall. Some business people will not deal with, or employ, people who turn up late. Why? If someone turns up late it's because they have an inadequate consciousness of time. They're not respecting their own time. They're also showing a lack of respect of other people's time. They show a lack of respect for your plans and consequently, the people around them are not considered important enough.

If you are someone who continually shows up late for meetings for friends, parties, lectures, and tutorials then you can't be trusted. It's as simple as that. If you say you will be somewhere at a certain time and you are not, then you cannot be trusted.

Obviously, accidents and medical emergencies excepted, there is no reason to turn up late. It's all about trust. Can I trust you to turn up as arranged? You told me you would, I took that as your intention, and yet you didn't turn up. Why should I believe anything else that you tell me?

Do you draw a distinction between saying that you will do something and making a promise to do the same thing? Both should produce the same results, yet making a sworn promise to meet at a certain time does tend to have a greater impact on the conscious mind and increases the likelihood of the appointment being met. But people need to trust your word and when you say you will do something, they expect that you will.

When asked to do something, do you appease people, telling them what you think they want to hear, just to make them happy? Do you secretly know that, whilst you will do your best, you really have a lot of other things to do… are not that organised and… they will have to be happy with the outcome? Which may be that you let them down.

"IT'S ALL ABOUT TRUST. CAN I TRUST YOU TO TURN UP AS ARRANGED?"

Being punctual and being obvious about it tends to focus people's minds. They will sooner or later get more organised when their meeting is with you. If however you will wait up to one hour for them to turn up, they may take longer to train.

So you need to make some decisions about how long you will give people beyond the set time. Let your friends know that you will wait 10 minutes and then you will do something else. This will focus their minds and they should start to treat your time with more respect.

Do you find yourself sometimes searching websites that provide good excuses for people who are late? Some people do: *I'm sorry I'm late, it's because... the bus was late... the train broke down... the alarm clock didn't go off... some friends came round last night and stayed longer than I wanted... the rain slowed me down?*

I know people who deliberately turn up half an hour late for meetings because they know the person they have arranged to meet is always at least half an hour late. How crazy is that? You need to learn to trust yourself to keep time commitments so that others, in turn, can trust you. You also need to consider your Plan B. What will you do if your friends don't turn up within your wait-time?

"I must govern the clock, not be governed by it."
— *Golda Meir*

You should not let other people be the cause of your wasted time. Punctuality is an obvious indicator that people can't really hide; they're either on time or not. Being early counts as being on time. So what else does it tell us if someone is habitually late?

- *they can't be trusted with the value of their time or yours*
- *they don't have an adequate respect for other people in general*
- *they lack integrity, honesty and are possibly self-centred*
- *they lack self-organisation*
- *they lack self-respect* and
- *someone whose word can't be trusted may also tell 'white lies' or worse.*

If you see yourself in some or the majority of the above list then I would encourage you to ask yourself this; is this sort of life working for you? If it is then that's fine and the rest of this book probably isn't for you, as it will need you to consider far more changes than you are prepared to undertake. I can assure you that, by valuing your time and that of others, as well as being punctual, you will get a massive beneficial change. It will affect your life positively including your outlook, optimism and your results. You will also start to get better outcomes from those around you who start to treat you more seriously.

As you start to focus on the management of your time, you will feel more powerful and organised. You will start to see those people around you who are wasting their time and yours. You will start to migrate towards more organised people and develop strategies to put this newly found time to better use. One of the benefits of valuing your time is that you end up with far more of it to use. So the question is, how are you going to put this time to good use?

Using your time well is quite easy. Here are some practical examples to make sure you squeeze every last minute from each day.

3.2 Timely travel

"Better three hours too soon than a minute too late."
— *William Shakespeare*

If you have ever turned up late for an important meeting, you've hopefully apologised, but now you are on the 'back foot'. You may feel that you've let yourself down and caused a lowering in your host's impression of you. If you don't feel guilty or humbled, then you have a long way to go and lots to learn about social interaction, integrity and honesty.

Being stuck in the tail of a car crash on the motorway that ends up making the evening news or taking an ill child to hospital for an emergency operation are reasonable excuses for being late, but stuck in rush-hour traffic, missing your regular bus / train, having a late night out the evening before etc. are just not good reasons for being late. In fact, it's usually best not to give an explanation.

The reason you were late is likely because you didn't make the meeting important enough to: get up earlier; get an earlier bus or train; or refrain from drinking the previous night. British businesses lose around £36 Billion annually through staff absence and the Monday hangover from a hard-played Sunday is a major contributor.

> "ONE OF THE BENEFITS OF VALUING YOUR TIME IS THAT YOU END UP WITH FAR MORE OF IT TO USE."

You do not want this sort of suspicion hanging over you at job interviews, especially as many larger companies will ask you to open your Facebook and Twitter accounts right there in the interview! What do your social accounts say about you... from an employer's perspective?

Timing your arrival to within minutes ensures that you don't spend time hanging around for others to arrive. However, this can lead to spectacular failures and so I always recommend setting off early.

If you often drive through rush-hour, you will find that there is a critical time at which setting off five minutes sooner will reduce travel time by up to 20 minutes and setting off five minutes later will cause you up to 20 or more minutes delay. People stick to patterns. If you can find a travel pattern that works for you, then you can manage your time to miss these inefficient journeys. Many professionals arrange their working day to either start and leave work early or to start and leave late, thereby avoiding the rush-hour traffic.

Being on time gives you power if the person you are seeing is late; you have the psychological upper-hand. Indeed, if you arrive early, you might be seen early. If you arrive late you might not be seen at all.

If you do arrive early, make sure you have some interesting emails or podcasts to listen to. Listening for 15 minutes to the lecture podcast on Alkaloid Chemistry / Genome Development / Modern Anaesthetic Techniques... or whatever your subject is, will keep you efficient, focused and ahead of the pack.

If you are going for a job interview, hot news in that sector can make an inspiring and impactful discussion with your interviewer. So plan to fill your time, whatever the circumstance – **fill** it, don't **kill** it.

3.3 Minimise interruptions

"If I know somebody is coming round, it is incredibly difficult for me to work because I'm waiting for this interruption — even the children's comings and goings are interruptions. Cake-making is a good way of coming out of that space."
— Rachel Cusk

To start with, you might have to lock yourself into your room, study in a different building on campus or on a different floor in the Library to your normal one. You may have to be quite ruthless until your friends and acquaintances get to see that your study-time is precious and non-negotiable. When you need to study, you need to study.

Whilst holed-up and working like a demon, your phone should be turned off. Whatever message people want to get to you (and it's usually trivial and not time-urgent), it can wait until the next 'Social time' or 'Communicate' slot comes around in your schedule (we'll be looking at daily schedules shortly).

Once you start laying down the rules by which you want to be treated, you soon learn who your friends are and those around you who are being disrespectful of your time. You will also find that the latter are largely disorganised and unfocused. They may be good fun at a party, but keep them away from you whilst you work.

By contrast, some of your friends will be as organised, if not more organised than you, or can work intensively for long periods of time. They will also want to exercise periodically, use energy, and mess-around as a break in their studies, just as you will want to do with yours. But unless you coordinate schedules or agree times when you are going to meet up, your friends are likely to cause you interruptions. So, for those friends of yours that are organised and dedicated, try to link your schedules so you finish studying at the same time.

If you use a different building or floor of your Library, away from people who you know, you will sometimes be interrupted by other students who are chatting, eating or drinking and using the study space casually. Confronting them can be intimidating, distracting and stressful, especially if they are regulars to that space and you are the hard-working interloper. One solution that you may consider to resolve this is to make a one-time visit to the admin office in the building, get an appropriate email address of someone who has responsibility for that space and, whilst the interruption progresses, send a polite email asking for an immediate and casual 'spot check'. It usually does the trick of dispersing troublemakers anonymously.

As you remain agile, moving from one quiet floor / building to another in search of the ideal study space, make sure you have your materials with you. With most campuses covered by Wi-Fi now, you should have all your electronic notes, lecture notes, slideshows, Word and Excel documents loaded up to either a Dropbox, Google Drive, SkyDrive or other cloud store (typically 5 to 25 GB for some students) or any resource you have through your university.

"WHILST HOLED-UP AND WORKING LIKE A DEMON, YOUR PHONE SHOULD BE TURNED OFF."

As an aside, with gigabytes of free space on offer, you have no excuse for carrying and losing your work on a memory stick. Indeed, memory sticks are one of the most commonly lost / forgotten items in computer labs. Many are handed in, but not all are.

Unfortunately, the value of the device is minor compared to the loss of the data you have lovingly crafted. Imagine keeping all your module work from several years on a single stick; reports, spreadsheets, photos, audio etc. and then losing it. Some students do... don't let it be you.

The problem of losing a memory stick can be doubly troubling especially if an unscrupulous student in a lower year on your course gets access to your work. Subtle re-writes of your work can easily get picked up by the automated **Turnitin** plagiarism checker and highlight you as the colluder (the 'providing' half) in an academic integrity case. Has this happened before? You bet it has.

In later chapters we look at being more focused, directional and intentional with your time. But first, let's take a look at your motives and drives in life. You should have a better understanding of time now, so let's take a generalised look at what makes you tick, what makes you happy. We'll even cover the sort of things you do that can lower your mood, as well as strategies for addressing unhappiness.

Many of the things you do in life will benefit you enormously, but everyone makes mistakes, perhaps doing things which they end up being embarrassed about for many weeks / months / years. So I want to introduce you to the concept of your personal **Life Values**. These are standards and directions in your life that are already largely set and, if you know what they are, can work to reinforce them. Doing things against our Life Values can be extremely upsetting. So you need to know what they are and how they can help you in your studies.

Let's get started on this journey of personal life values exploration. If you haven't done this life-changing exercise before, then just prepare yourself for some real thinking and a few hours of deliberation. Done well, it can take a while and is a very worthwhile exercise.

CHAPTER 4
PERSONAL VALUES

"Here are the values that I stand for: honesty, equality, kindness, compassion, treating people the way you want to be treated and helping those in need. To me, those are traditional values."

— Ellen DeGeneres

Values are what we hold dear, whether we are consciously aware of them or not. Valued activity charges our batteries and provides fulfilment. When an activity takes us away from our values, we may feel sad, depressed or unfulfilled. Doing something which is against our values can leave us ashamed or embarrassed for a long time. So finding out what our Life Values are is an important task. They aren't obvious, but finding or re-affirming your own Life Values is like meeting an old friend... comforting and positive. Values are descriptions of ways of doing things.

Life Values fall into different categories, but they basically represent a metaphorical direction of travel. For example, if we have a value relating to being a *Good and Loving Son / Daughter*, then giving a parent a quick ring every few weeks to say that everything is going well and that you are having fun, will support and affirm that value. It will provide you with a good feeling, a job well done. If you haven't visited or communicated with them in any form for six or eight weeks, you might start feeling guilty. Indeed, sometimes guilt and depression from irregular contact will actively stop you calling, keeping you from doing the things you know you need to do. I know, I was that son at university... I was having so much fun that I assumed there would be no worry on their part. Wrong!

Try this exercise: think about two major events in your life, one good and the other bad. Just have a think and find two that really stand out. For the good one, what were your feelings? Try and relive those emotions right now. Why was it good? What were your Values in relation to the event and can you determine if you were moving towards them?

For the bad event, it is likely that what happened had you moving away from your Life Values. Can you see what your values were and how the event moved you away from them? How did you feel; were you guilty or worried? What would you have had to do at the time to turn that experience around so that you were moving towards your values?

Let's look at two examples and tease out the Life Values in them to show you what I mean.

A Good Event. You used to swim regularly at school and have only recently taken it up again at uni. You are now swimming half a mile, twice a week, and you feel great about it. You are fit and healthy and loving the feel-good endorphin rush it provides.

This activity is moving you positively along your Health Value which provides you with a fit and healthy body.

A Bad Event. You left a girlfriend / boyfriend at home when you came to university and, whilst you have moved on emotionally, you never finished the relationship properly. You know you owe them an explanation... that difficult '*I don't love you anymore*' conversation. You don't want to upset them, you don't want to expose yourself to their distress, there's a strong element of cowardice on your part... it's really messy... so you avoid it.

It's made worse when, on a Christmas shopping trip to your home town, you accidentally meet and their friends tell you what a *$%!&£ you are. The nagging and gnawing at your guilty conscience is a result of you moving in the wrong direction along your Partner Values. The best way to resolve this is to take the difficult and personal approach and tell it like it is. Your Partner Values will require you to explain it from a position of understanding and empathy. Be honest, do your best (consult with good friends for advice), give it closure and learn from the experience.

> **"One thing I didn't understand in life was that I had $100,000,000 in the bank and I couldn't buy happiness. I had everything: mansions, yachts, Ferraris, Lamborghinis, but I was depressed. I didn't know where I fitted in. But then I found family and friends and I learned the value of life."**
> — *Vanilla Ice*

We all have different life experiences and some of the situations we find ourselves in don't always feel comfortable. Sometimes it can take quite a long time to get back to feeling good after a bad event. One advantage that thinking about your Life Values provides is that you don't need to have had a good or privileged upbringing, you just need to focus yourself towards your Values and you will feel happy and good about yourself once again.

Values tend not to change much during a person's lifetime, so once you find what your Life Values are, you'll probably be okay sticking to them.

Values can be categorised into eight different areas (Value Domains) of your life:

- *Family relationships – parents, grandparents, brothers, sisters*
- *Social relationships – friends, acquaintances, flatmates, next door neighbours*
- *Partner relationships – husband / wife, partner, lover, girl / boyfriend*
- *Spirituality – religious, self-awareness, self-reflection*
- *Work / career – part-time hours, internships, placements, graduate job, professional bodies*
- *Study and personal development – lectures, assignments, exams, self-development, meditation*
- *Health – exercise, strength, stamina, flexibility*
- *Hobbies and creativity – pastimes, fun, pleasure, creativity.*

It would be great if you could take some time out from reading this book now and do an exercise which looks at your personal values. Why? Because doing things which are valued by you will make you feel fulfilled. You also get to see that doing things which work against your Values will make you unhappy, sad or even depressed. Depression and inactivity are two of the biggest stumbling blocks for some students and they can stop your study and degree progression in its tracks.

By knowing your Life Values, you will be able to convince yourself that the various tasks you have been putting off are well worth doing because they will move you along your valued path and make you happier. Whilst it would be great if you could tackle all eight domains at once, realistically, you will have pressing demands from your course and so assessing three or four of the most pressing areas is recommended initially.

Firstly you need to evaluate yourself against each of the domains in question. Work up a few values statements for each of the areas in question and then rank them to see which ones are causing you the most problems. Do this by giving each value statement a score, something from a 1 to 5 range where 1 represents minimal change and 5 is a dire need for work.

The exercise can be done electronically in the spreadsheet by duplicating and renaming the blank *Your Life Values* tab or by printing off the blank page as many times as you like. The spreadsheet can be downloaded from the **MaxYourDegree website** (www.maxyourdegree.com).

The spreadsheet has three tabs:

- *Values Keywords*

- *Your Life Values* and

- *Example Life Values.*

The first has an A to Z list of values hidden behind the drop-down arrow on each of the letters. This is a huge list of values which is great if you are stuck for ideas. **Figure 1** shows a scrolling list of value ideas for the letter A.

MAX YOUR DEGREE

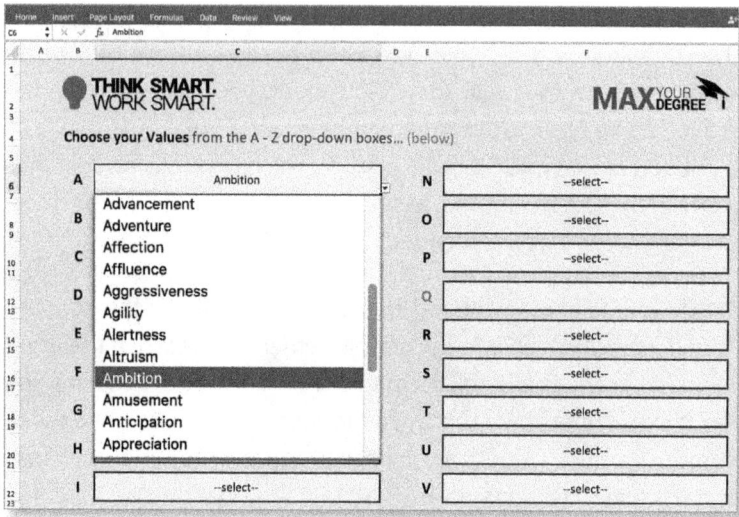

Figure 1. *Alphabetical list of values on the 'Values Keywords' tab*

The values you write out should be important to you. If you have had a tough childhood, this task may be difficult, especially in the Family, Social and Spirituality domains.

So here's the best way to tackle it; just imagine that *you can have your life any way you want* and then write the Life Value on the respective sheet. Don't let the past stop you from writing down what is important to you or what you would like to value in the future. These values are what you hold dear, the way you aspire to live your life. Use the A to Z lists for ideas if you get stuck.

To help you, the spreadsheet has an example for each 'Value Domain' (***Example Life Values*** tab) and it may take you half an hour or a whole weekend to get the form filled out just the way you want. If you get stuck and have some close family or friends to hand, it's worth consulting them as they probably know you better than you know yourself. Remember though, this is about you and your values, not about how they see you.

Some of the values you might recognise are given below and **Figure 2** shows part of the example form:

- *Being reliable and supportive to your friends*
- *Being loving, caring and communicative family member to parents, grandparents, siblings*
- *Being a valuable member of the team at work*
- *Being fit and healthy*
- *Being a considerate caring neighbour to your immediate and elderly neighbours*
- *Being financially independent*
- *Being the best student you can be* and
- *Being a self-reflective developer, constantly open to new approaches to study and life.*

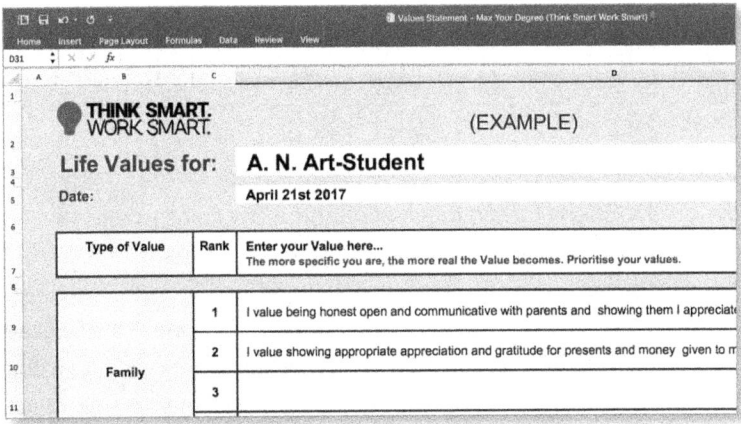

Figure 2. *Part of the 'Example Life Values' form.*

There are two basic barriers which might stop you from achieving actions along your valued path: one is internal, the other external.

Internal barriers include your thoughts, feelings, memories of experiences, worries about things that may or may not happen, physical feelings, anxiety, tiredness, lack of motivation and imagery (dreams and nightmares). Internal barriers are your own worst enemy!

External barriers are things like the amount of time, money and opportunity that you have. Most entrepreneurs would of course argue that it doesn't matter what time and money you currently have, you can become a multi-millionaire (or achieve anything you want) by using the time that you have to take advantage of an abundance of opportunities.

> "..DOING THINGS WHICH ARE VALUED BY YOU WILL MAKE YOU FEEL FULFILLED... DOING THINGS WHICH WORK AGAINST YOUR VALUES WILL MAKE YOU UNHAPPY, SAD OR EVEN DEPRESSED."

We tend to spend far too much of our time attending to the internal barriers, such as thoughts and feelings, because changing external barriers is challenging and requires planning, action and effort. We'll be looking at thoughts and feelings in **Book 2** of the **MaxYourDegree** series *'Healthy Body & Mind'*, and in particular, developing a strong sense of emotional resilience. Solving the internal barrier issue is one of the best ways of making fabulous positive changes in your life... with minimal effort. It is well worth a read if you suffer from emotional ups and downs or just want to increase your emotional resilience.

So, let's recap the learning you have done in this book so far:

- *you are putting greater value on your time (something like £36/hr) and wasting much less of it... allowing more time for study and fun activities*
- *you have learnt the importance of turning up on time for your commitments. You become more trusted by your friends and get better treatment from those around you... you become a better role model*
- *you are able to accurately judge how reliable someone is via their time-keeping* and
- *you have thought long and hard about the values you hold dear in your life. You have made them real and perhaps discovered much about yourself in the process. All your future work and interactions should move you along your valued path.*

Well done! You should now feel clearer about your life (or at least see a better path through your degree). However, there's something missing; we haven't looked at your goals yet. What is it that you want to achieve?

Perhaps your goals are not as well-defined and obvious as they could be. You see, it's only when you know where you are going in life that you can you judge your progress at any moment. Also, you need to be able to remind yourself regularly what your goals are because they will help you get through difficult times. You need a reminder of your ambitions... you need to keep your eyes on the prize.

So we are now going to look at Goal Setting. This process defines your short-, medium- and long-term goals. It uses the **SMART** approach. If you haven't already planned your future in step-by-step detail, then this next process is going to be quite an eye-opener. It's not about defining the end-product that you will become, more about helping you break down the daily, weekly, monthly and yearly challenges in to bite-size and do-able pieces of work. Time to work out your goals.

CHAPTER 5
GOAL SETTING

"A goal without a plan is like an empty wish."
— *Antoine de Saint-Exupéry*

You wouldn't get on a long-distance jet or coach, the first one that you came to, and travel until you were kicked off. What would be the point ... other than drunken behaviour, a student bet or a rag-week stunt? You might end up somewhere you didn't want to be or didn't like. What would you do when you got there and how would you get back... assuming you wanted to, or were able?

So are you guilty of doing the same thing with your life? Most of us (probably close to 95%) are stumbling headlong into the unknown future, knowing only vague future goals: I want a degree, I want to have two kids, I want to be a Biochemist, I want a holiday in the sun this summer.

You probably know your short-term goals; pass the upcoming exams, have a great summer holiday, make some new friends, have a great time at Glastonbury etc. But what if you could have a strategy where you decided on your short-, medium- and long-term goals, right now? The idea here is that you focus on some ambitious targets then break the necessary steps down in to easy chunks. That way, you envisage what you want to do or be, create a simple and do-able plan and then execute the steps. You achieve exactly what you planned in the time allotted. Could this radical method work? Of course, welcome to the *5-year plan* approach.

> **"There is nothing wrong with change, if it is in the right direction. To improve is to change, so to be perfect is to change often."**
> — Winston Churchill

So what do you want, what sort of detail can you think up, and how much effort is it worth putting in to this daydream? Because, let's face it, it probably won't happen, right? ***Wrong!***

Your goals will be achieved, you are going to make it happen. The process of writing your goals on paper will get you 50% of the way. All you have to do then is make it happen.

So, just imagine that you can have exactly what you want, you just have to plan for it. You see, we dream about things that our subconscious knows we can make happen, and dreaming is the first step of planning; you need your ideas.

So here's what you need to do to get exactly where you want to be; you need to set realistic goals. I'm going to take you through the Goal Setting process, to start you thinking about what you actually want to achieve and how you are going to get there.

The process is easy once it's broken down into stages and the first step is to categorise the goals in to the same areas as our Value Domains (chapter 4, Personal Values). The descriptions have been fleshed-out a little to give you a greater sense of the goals you might engage in:

- *Family relationships – parents, grandparents, brothers, sisters, fostering, caring*
- *Social relationships – friends, acquaintances, flatmates, next door neighbours, charity, volunteering*
- *Partner relationships – husband / wife, partner, lover, girl / boyfriend*
- *Spirituality – religious, self-awareness, self-reflection, attitude, brain challenges, mindset*
- *Work / career – part-time job, internships, placements, graduate job, professional bodies, employee or employer, entrepreneur, freelance, industry accolades, savings, stocks and shares, mortgage and debt*
- *Study and personal development – lectures, assignments, revision, exams, degree and classification, Masters/Doctorate, courses, retraining*
- *Health – exercise, strength, stamina, fitness, flexibility, endurance*
- *Hobbies and creativity – pastimes, fun, pleasure, art, writing, performance, clubs.*

We should ideally have a goal or two in each of the eight areas. This ensures we have a full and balanced life and avoids the workaholic or hedonistic excesses that cause us Life Value conflicts. However, that's a lot of work, so to get started we need to think **small** and **achievable**, then grow the range of our goals as we become more confident.

The **SMART** approach to goal setting has been used successfully for many years. It's quite easy to use and the letters stand for **S**mall, **M**easurable, **A**chievable, **R**elevant and **T**imely. The **SMART** approach is all about making the tasks small enough to be started, relevant to your life's aims, achievable and timely. Different authors have additional words for each of the five letters, so here are many of them:

- *S*mall – What is the goal? Make it bite-size small, significant and as specific as possible

- *M*easurable – Make sure it is meaningful and that you can measure it... then you know when you have have arrived

- *A*chievable – Don't set yourself up for a fall. Make it achievable and action-orientated. Impossible goals are... impossible!

- *R*elevant – It has to be relevant to your life goals as well as rewarding

- *T*imely – At what time do you intend to achieve your goal? Make sure it is trackable.

"..IMAGINE THAT YOU CAN HAVE EXACTLY WHAT YOU WANT... YOU JUST HAVE TO PLAN FOR IT."

The eight goals areas are included in a spreadsheet and can be downloaded from the **MaxYourDegree** *website*. Search the Downloads area for the SMART Goals files.

The SMART Goals spreadsheet, includes eight tabs; one for each of the eight goal areas (above). There is an additional tab showing an example layout for the Health domain (***Example Health*** tab) and a separate blank sheet (**Blank Goals Sheet** tab) if you want to write it all out for yourself.

A good starting point is to choose just two or three of the eight domains and write down one goal in each of the short-, medium- and long-term areas. That's up to nine goals spread over three areas. As you get better at the process, you can extend your goal objectives. An example can be seen in **Figure 3** for the example showing **Health Goals**.

The idea ultimately is that you work through each of the eight areas putting in as many short-, medium- and long-term goals as you can, but ideally at least one in each. This can take a few months to work up to, so don't rush the process. Do not underestimate how long this work will take, nor how powerful it will be at focusing your attention on what is truly important to you!

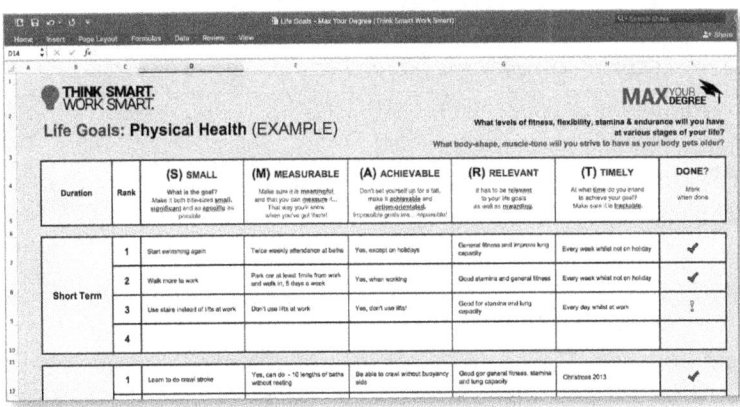

Figure 3. *'Typical Life Goals' sheet completed. 'Health Goals' Example...*

By undertaking this work on your goals, you will cause a radical shift in the way you approach life and the way it turns out, not least by making you a more reflective person. Look really hard and put some effort in to this, it will revolutionise your world!

The main elements of each form are the five columns (S, M, A, R and T, as above) and the three rows representing duration. But how short is Short and how long is Long?

The duration of each period is somewhat open to interpretation, but for an undergraduate degree, even starting in your first year, the following might seem as being appropriate:

- **Short-term:** *current date up to one year or to the start of the next academic year (to include summer holidays)*
- **Medium-term:** *anything from 12 to 18 months (or to the end of your degree), perhaps including getting a graduate job*
- **Long-term:** *ideally these would be more aspirational career or work-life balance goals such as retire to the seaside at 50 after selling company for £10 Million. However, as an undergraduate, you should cast your eye no further than the early years of your first job; in say two to four year's time.*

"Setting goals is the first step in turning the invisible into the visible."

— Anthony Robbins

The duration is up to you, but keeping the goals in each of the three periods seemingly do-able is the main idea. You need to make each goal seem achievable; otherwise you will be looking at your goals knowing that you couldn't possibly achieve that amount of success. Don't set yourself up for a fall before you commence!

Making a start on your tasks is always difficult, so I've broken them down in to easy stages:

1 *Download the Life Goals spreadsheet from the* **MaxYourDegree website** *and open it up. There are links for different file formats, so pick yours carefully. Have a look at the content on all 10 tabs*

2 *Take a look at the 'Example Health' tab and see the sort of goals outlined there to give you an idea of the wording and what is expected*

3 *Either working electronically within the spreadsheet or from the printed pages, take up to three of the eight goals sheets in turn and work through each one*

4 *Make sure you have at least one goal for the short-, medium- and long-term in your chosen sections*

5 *For each goal description, add pertinent details for the four remaining columns: measurement, action-orientation, relevancy and the date when will you will have achieved this goal*

6 *If you are just starting out with this process or worried about progress, just pick the three most important ones and tackle the short goals first. Then move on to tackling the other goals*

7 *Sit back, relax and reflect on what you have just achieved. You have just done a bit of magic. If asked to write an action plan for your life, you would likely have struggled, but you have just broken down your future achievements over the next four to five years into bite-size chunks. Your future life is starting to take shape in black and white.*

The difficulty you will now have is putting it all in to practice. You ideally need to develop strategies, tactics and procedures to do all this new stuff, but that's just a matter of modifying your behaviours and expanding the anticipation of your outcomes. Often we limit our futures by not having the confidence in ourselves to achieve. These negative beliefs can be very powerful... but they do need to go. As you work on your goals and achieve them, you will start to trust yourself more and to further open up your outlook on the future.

You should hold on to the good behaviours and habits that get you to your goals faster. The more you do, the better your results. Ultimately, you can establish new behaviours and expectations which become your norm; you will learn that you can achieve your aims, whatever they are. You can have fun with this system by being ambitious and then making sure you succeed.

Controlling unhelpful habits and learning new behaviours is dealt with in some detail in the second book in the **MaxYourDegree** series, *'Healthy Body & Mind'*.

You do need to be careful about how specific you are with your goals. The problem with goals like: *I want to be a millionaire* or *I want a gorgeous wife / husband*, is that they aren't quite specific enough and we need some preparatory steps that will get us there.

"Obstacles are those frightful things you see when you take your eyes off your goal."
— Henry Ford

One reason why we fail to achieve goals, or fall off our goal path, is because they are just too big for us to achieve right now. It can be quite demoralising to view a goal as being too big to be achieved. The steps need breaking down in size so we can see our way.

Q. *How do you walk a thousand mile journey?*

A. *One step at a time.*

So you should have three goal tracks sketched out. Let's look at an ambitious example for some of these differently timed goals. This is either the life plan of someone who knows what they want or of someone who is a wishful thinker... it's not the ideal student plan by a long way, so make sure you read the section that follows.

Example of an overly-ambitious plan.

The long-term: PhD by 25, manage a large company, self-made millionaire at 40, retirement by 50, husband / wife and three children, £M home. These are the headline goals.

The medium-term goals are major stopping off points along the way: attain 1st Class Honours, have a six months round the world trip, commence funded PhD, invent widget / product / service / App and launch in spare time, work for a Blue Chip company, earning more than £75k by age 30.

Short-term goals: get part-time job within two weeks for 14 hours/ week, achieve minimum 70% in upcoming assignments / exams, plan route of six month holiday.

You might have an incredible burning ambition and can see yourself in elements of this example, but for many students, the goals need to be much smaller and attainable... more believable.

So let's have a look at a five year plan from the second year of an undergraduate degree course. This student is ambitious and knows a *First Class Honours* degree is feasible.

Example of a Student 5-year plan

Long-term: Working for an international Blue Chip company on their graduate scheme. Opportunities for travel with work. Purchase Buy-To-Let property which is managed by a Lettings Agency as part of private pension planning. Full Member of Chartered Institute.

Medium-term: work for a large company during the placement year, get part-time hours in final year with same company, attain a *First*. Travel and work in Australia for three months.

Short-term: start all assignments early, manage study time well, attend all lectures / tutorials, hand assignments in on time, attain min 70% in everything, work as a University Helper, spend 4hrs per week volunteering at local care home, attend placement job training and have excellent CV, engage with placement staff fully, chase down and research the best placement jobs.

Perhaps the second example feels more attainable and real to you. It might look like quite a stretch to attain those goals from where you are now, but remember, this is all about creating your bold plan and not working to someone else's.

"Having an aim is the key to achieving your best."
— Henry J. Kaiser

You might not have access to a placement job, but this could be swapped with a year out in industry, volunteering, working gap-year, a series of internships or other similar activities if this proves to be useful for your progression.

This process gives you some real, attainable and bite-size goals. If you are interested in looking at money and employment (both as an undergraduate and afterwards) you might be interested in looking at the third planned book in the **MaxYourDegree** series about work and careers.

It is important to be as specific as possible with goals. In the overly-ambitious plan above, two of the goals (millionaire and wife plus three children) weren't adequately specific. So let's look at each one in turn to show you what I mean:

- what do we mean by being a millionaire? Earning a million pounds before tax or after? Is it having a million pounds in the bank? Is it having a company turnover of a million or a market capitalisation of a million pounds? You need to be quite specific. To have a million pounds in the bank, after tax and living expenses, implies high earnings and a concerted savings effort

- the husband / wife and three children can easily turn into an Ex a year later. The children may not be yours (step-children, adopted, fostered), so you do need to be very specific.

"You've got to know what you want. This is central to acting on your intentions. When you know what you want, you realize that all there is left then is time management. You'll manage your time to achieve your goals because you clearly know what you're trying to achieve in your life."

— Patch Adams

The more specific you are with your goals, the more solid the ideas become in your conscious and subconscious mind. You want to get to the point where, without thinking, you will naturally be taking goal-directed steps instead of wasting your time going in other directions.

You will likely struggle on many parts of the goal-setting exercise because you've possibly never had any thoughts about being so focussed and determined. This may even be the first time that you have been asked to think about your future in real depth and especially about your goals. It will probably take between two hours and two days (a weekend) to do this work and it is so worth the effort.

If you have supportive parents or other members of your family, seek their guidance. Someone you trust and love and who is in touch with the deeper *you* is perfectly placed to help you with this. I strongly recommend printing the sheets out to discuss it with them. And remember, this is all about you.

"THE MORE SPECIFIC YOU ARE WITH YOUR GOALS, THE MORE SOLID THE IDEAS BECOME IN YOUR CONSCIOUS AND SUBCONSCIOUS MIND."

Your goals are what you want to do and achieve. They are targets that reflect your behaviour towards your valued direction. Your achievements and milestones indicate that you are moving your life in the right direction... as planned. Don't make filling out the forms a race and don't scrimp on the information. Give the task the time it deserves.

You are now an expert in valuing your time, you know what value directions bring you joy (and pain) and you now have a plan of activities mapped out for the next few years.

Completing each of the short-term goals brings your medium-term goals in to focus, but where do you start with organising your daily life to ensure you do the work involved for those short-term tasks? It starts with a combination of managing both your time and your tasks.

The use of a To-Do list, in conjunction with a diary forms the basis of what we cover in the next chapter — *scheduling*. So let's get right on and work out, in a step-by-step fashion, how the schedule is going to revolutionise your work output and make you in to a super-smart and productive student. Read on...

MAX YOUR DEGREE

CHAPTER 6
GETTING STARTED

"The key is not to prioritize what's on your schedule, but to schedule your priorities."
— Stephen Covey

You will see that we are taking progressive steps here; valuing time, being punctual and trustworthy, defining your values and setting achievable goals. You should have created many more hours in your week with which to do something more purposeful. So what are you going to do with them? Perhaps accelerate your studies, complete those short term tasks, do a range of must-do, should-do and could-do's that make life so wonderful.

The problem is that there's a roadblock in front of many tasks and it's called **procrastination**. So let's first take a look at procrastination, dissect it and generate strategies for overcoming it.

6.1 Procrastination

"The essence of procrastination lies in not doing what you think you should be doing, a mental contortion that surely accounts for the great psychic toll the habit takes on people. This is the perplexing thing about procrastination: although it seems to involve avoiding unpleasant tasks, indulging in it generally doesn't make people happy."

— James Surowiecki

Without strategies and a cast-iron will, humans are natural procrastinators and given freedom to do just what we want, we tend to do just what we want. It usually includes a large component of nothing much or messing around. Playing and being absorbed in computer games is a good example of a modern distraction, as is social interaction on Facebook, Twitter, Instagram, Pinterest... (it's a long list).

The good news is that we humans are also fairly good at following procedures, rules and guides; especially when we have some ownership in their creation and know that they are good for our overall progression.

Since the use of time is a predominant factor in personal success, we are going to use scheduling to help us. It combines the mechanical statements of what needs doing (shopping lists are possibly the closest you've come to these useful things already) with time slots which have a start time, finish time and hence a duration.

So let's cut to the chase here, you already know that:

- *if you can put it off, you will. This is procrastination*
- *the longer you put something off, the more it hangs around and the more you make your molehill into a mountain*
- *procrastination makes us unhappy and takes the shine off a normal day*
- *you can always find a different (very important) job to do instead of the one you need to do*
- *it's very easy to convince yourself, and others, that you are being busy* and
- *you will eventually have to do the thing you have been avoiding, or suffer the consequences (low assignment marks, a formal penalty or risk someone's wrath).*

Procrastination is useful, it does serve a purpose; it stops us having to do the things we don't want to do. It may work well for you... today. But, procrastination serves as a barrier to living up to our values and reduces fulfilment in the longer term.

Below is a list of procrastination-breaking strategies. One or more may help you to do the things you should be doing:

1. *Set your goals and still procrastinating? Break your goals down into smaller bite-size chunks so they become easy and do-able*

2. *Change of scene. If your bedroom / flat isn't working for you (flat-mate interruptions, noisy music), spend more time in the Department, Library, a friend's house*

3. *Write down your calendar / time-line with milestones and deadlines. A visual picture of time works well for many students*

4   *When you procrastinate, you are probably spending time on... Twitter, Facebook, email, text, surfing, YouTube, TV, eating etc. Note what you do when you are avoiding your tasks and just make a point of not doing these activities. Set some time aside for these pleasurable activities, and work the remainder of the time. Get rid of distractions*

5   *Hang-out with top students, they are the hard-working ones, they are valuable to you. They have what you want... tenacity, consistency of effort and success. You will have to match their performance to be accepted in their circle, but their good behaviours will rub off on you and you will improve your performance*

6   *Study buddy. Share learning, revision, goals and other important tasks and challenge each other. Chat about the course content regularly. Exchange problems and answers frequently — learn from each other*

7   *Proclaim your ambitions. Tell your friends that you want a First Class Honours degree. True friends will support you and you will have that extra motivation to make sure it happens*

8   *Make friends with students on your course on a higher year. They've been there, done it all and can advise accordingly. Moral support from someone who has been through your current difficulties is a big help in difficult times*

9   *Timing. The only perfect time is to do that thing right now. You know that things are never perfect, and often,* **Good enough is good enough.** *There's no point risking a 72% mark on an assignment only to try to perfect it and hand in late... to be capped at 40%.*

10 *Carpe Diem - seize the day. Do it now... just do it... now.*

So why not throw all your jobs on to a list, set the start and finish time for each and get it all done... out of the way... off your chest? Why not? Probably because it involves work and many people are comfortable keeping the impossible, difficult, involved and boring tasks at bay.

You see, you are wired-up to avoid doing things that you don't want to do. The kicker is this: it is simply easier on your life (goals, happiness, achievements... you name the measure) to get the job done as soon as possible and get it out of the way.

So, the answer to many of your problems is to run your life from a schedule. Scheduling time is one of the main work practices of successful people. So let's have a look at the **schedule**.

6.2 The Schedule

"A schedule defends from chaos and whim. It is a net for catching days. It is a scaffolding on which a worker can stand and labor with both hands at sections of time."
— Annie Dillard

At its most basic form, a schedule is a chronological list of activities set against timeslots. If you are a believer in lists, you will appreciate that not everything on the list gets done in a day.

Sometimes the big / difficult tasks get left until tomorrow and sometimes you will even do insignificant things that aren't on your list, as a means of procrastination. You then get to add them to your list... so that you can immediately cross them off and make your list (and your day) look better than it really is.

But what about the difficult tasks that didn't get done? They were left because they weren't timed or planned, there was no apparent urgency to do them or there was inadequate time committed to getting the job done. Hello scheduling!

"SCHEDULING TIME IS ONE OF THE MAIN WORK PRACTICES OF SUCCESSFUL PEOPLE."

There are certainties to your daily life; get out of bed, wash, have breakfast, wash teeth, travel to campus, attend lectures and tutorials, eat meals, return home, go to bed. In a 24-hour day, where you sleep a solid eight hours, that leaves 16 to fill. The above list of certainties will account for between four to 10 hours in a given day, so what about the remaining hours?

You could fill them with; meet friends, extended lunch / dinner, social networking, email, computer games, drinking, socialising. In fact the list of alternative things to do is almost endless. You may even be a creative expert at finding stuff to do other than what you should be doing.

So this is where the schedule comes in. The good thing about it is that you get to make your own schedule. You put the things on there that you want to get done. You have ownership and so you get the pleasure of doing these things and crossing them off.

THINK SMART. WORK SMART.

Working through and completing a daily schedule of things that you need to do is a fabulous feeling! The nasty jobs get done and you have time to have fun afterwards.

I do my own scheduling by creating a vertical column of half-hour slots then fill them with things I have to do, things I need to do and things I want to do (Figure 4). Everything has its time: eating, travel, lectures, tutorials, visiting the library, meetings with fellow students or staff, answering emails and making phone calls. In fact, (almost) everything you do needs to be on the schedule. It's a very formal structure and a copy can be obtained from the **MaxYourDegree** *website* (in the Downloads area called Schedules) so that you can alter it at will. Visit the Downloads area for this and other useful study asset files.

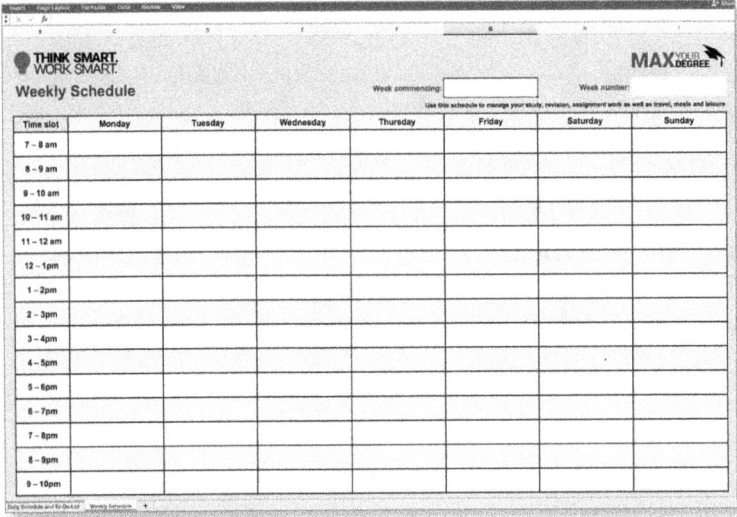

Figure 4. *A blank weekly schedule.*

GETTING STARTED   67

Whether you create your weekly schedule electronically on the spreadsheet or print off blank forms and complete with a pen, it's up to you. You could even use a mobile App to achieve the same results, there are many available (see chapter 9). The important thing is that you allocate the jobs you know need doing to the schedule, then do them when their time comes up.

6.3 Living with a Schedule

I have found from experience that the most difficult part of scheduling is filling out the weekly or daily form and not, as you might expect, doing the tasks themselves.

There's a magical linkage between intending to do a difficult task, committing it to the schedule and actually getting it done. It really is like magic.

Completing the schedule is when the difficult decisions are made and where the determination to do your tasks stems from. The rest is easy... kind of.

"Time management is an oxymoron. Time is beyond our control, and the clock keeps ticking regardless of how we lead our lives. Priority management is the answer to maximizing the time we have."
—*John C. Maxwell*

Because a difficult task may have been several weeks or months in your mind, you tend to forget how long it will take to complete the task, in reality. Your mountains usually are molehills and you will soon find out when you start tackling them that the task-duration is a lot less than you had feared. However, some tasks will take far longer than you had allotted, perhaps because you had not envisaged the research or detailed level of work expected of you. So here are a few pointers about your schedule;

- *fill in tomorrow's schedule, in full, at least the day / evening before. If you leave it until you wake up, your mind will already have justified skipping those early morning slots, wasting time that is gone forever*
- *make a commitment at least one day a week to get out of bed sooner than you would normally. Why not try getting up at 7:00am or earlier on Mondays? This will have a serious impact on your habits the previous evening and it sets the tone for the rest of the week*
- *fill in all the: get washed / dressed; breakfast; teeth; lunch; dinner and travel slots to see what is left*
- *now add in lecture, tutorial and supervisor / tutor meetings. I am constantly amazed that, having had a series of ping-pong emails with students to arrange a meeting during the week to discuss problems, the set time passes without the student appearing. Sometimes they are an hour late, sometimes they just don't appear at all. You likely have a smartphone with a scheduler – start to use it. If not, at least use the Alarm function*
- *assess the remaining gaps in relation to time needed for: writing up notes, preparation for assignments, revision for examinations. Now commit timeslots to these*
- *you also need to allocate slots for cleaning and tidying your room. Yes, you really need to do this. A tidy environment leads to a tidy mind; more on this later*
- *don't forget cooking, shopping, washing-up, washing and ironing. All those chores build up daily and if they aren't done, will gnaw and nag away at your happiness, and*

- don't forget the good things (how could you!): socialising, computer games, social networking, cinema. By putting these on your schedule you are rewarding yourself for the hard work you are doing and limiting their propensity to eat up your valuable time. The good thing is that if you want to spend more time on a particular activity, you get to choose to do this, thereby eliminating internal conflict. Just commit it to the schedule.

> *"I love deadlines. I like the whooshing sound they make as they fly by."*
> — Douglas Adams

There is one major psychological reason for keeping to a schedule, especially when you are conflicted or pressured by many subjects, assignments, revision and exam requirements. As pressures build throughout the academic year, it is quite easy to become distracted.

It can become difficult to concentrate and focus on the topic at hand because so many other demands are wanting to take their place. Your mind hops from one seemingly impossible deadline to another. You can easily start to suffer panic and anxiety. The schedule cuts across all this conflict.

If Monday morning 10am to 11am states *Revise Inorganic Chemistry*, then you can relax in the notion that you were in a sound and logical frame of mind when you completed the schedule. So you can forget all about the other conflicting tasks until their individual time slots come around.

This is a great way of de-cluttering your mind - offloading the worry of other tasks. In fact, the constant nagging of other work will eat away at your concentration and confidence on the task at hand, another reason why we tend to work at less than 100%. Scheduling is the single most important activity you can do to boost your success at studying and meeting those short term goals.

Perhaps you need to be able to value your time before you can see the sense and benefits, but scheduling will encourage you to have the mentality of doing the things you need to do in order to do the things you want and like to do.

Much of this has to do with being in-the-moment and stopping tasks from dragging on. I don't know anyone who enjoys their tasks mounting up; however, your role as a student (if you didn't know it already) is to manage an ever-increasing workload with strict deadlines. This book is all about working smarter and not necessarily harder, so do yourself an enormous favour and learn that these tasks go on the schedule - and they get done!

Sometimes you need to psyche yourself up to doing an arduous task. If so, just print out next week's schedule and put it on there. Set it up for a few days in the future. Just make sure it goes onto the schedule and I promise you, the timeslot will come around, the task will get done and you will feel enormous satisfaction.

The benefit and emotional release of completing daily tasks is proportional to the task difficulty and the length of time you have been procrastinating. For example, it might be September and you haven't yet thanked your Gran or Aunty for your last Christmas present. Just put it on the schedule, give her a ring or send a letter and solve that particular nagging issue. Better late than never, as they say, and whilst family always remember, they're very quick to forgive. You might even get a Christmas present next time around.

6.4 The ups and downs of a Schedule

"Productivity is never an accident. It is always the result of a commitment to excellence, intelligent planning, and focused effort."

— Paul J Meyer

When I started scheduling, I was struck by the amount of task repetition; *get out of bed, wash, breakfast, travel, supper, get ready for bed, sleep.* Sometimes they seem so obvious that they are not worth scheduling. A lot of these tasks can be repeated across days and weeks. A good idea is to edit the downloaded spreadsheet file (from the **MaxYourDegree** *website*) and put in the recurring entries. Just schedule them in, it will make your life easier.

It is very important that you schedule getting out of bed, travelling to university, mealtimes and going to bed. These are the anchors that keep you on the right path, keep you fuelled and stop you procrastinating.

> "[SCHEDULING]... A GREAT WAY OF DE-CLUTTERING YOUR MIND, BY OFFLOADING THE WORRY OF OTHER TASKS."

I have had several students tell me about their sleeping problems; not being able to sleep when they go to bed, lying awake for hours, waking up too early full of stress or wanting to stay in bed until lunchtime to compensate. Doing the right things at the right time, as per your schedule, will keep you on the right path. If you

THINK SMART. WORK SMART.

do have issues with sleep, get a hold of the second book in this **MaxYourDegree** series *'Healthy Body & Mind'*. You have some work in front of you, but it's just about getting back to a normal healthy rhythm of life.

As you become experienced in scheduling, you find certain benefits. If you always get up at 7am on weekdays but inadvertently sleep in one day, you will be rushing around to catch up to your schedule. This can be a good thing because it really focuses the mind and it is important that you find your scheduling to be helpful. But don't worry, if you miss something out, just add it to tomorrow's schedule.

> ## "SCHEDULING IS THE SINGLE MOST IMPORTANT ACTIVITY YOU CAN DO TO BOOST YOUR SUCCESS AT STUDYING AND MEETING THOSE SHORT TERM GOALS."

Q. *How do you eat an elephant?*

A. *One mouthful at a time.*

Some of the tasks you face will seem huge; exam revision for six subjects or completing three assignments for next week, for example. But the beauty of scheduling is that you chip away at the essential tasks in 30 or 60 minute consecutive slots and then reward yourself with a nourishing activity such as coffee with a friend, reading a chapter of a novel or chilling in the sun.

GETTING STARTED

With scheduling, you are constantly estimating how long tasks will take, as well as receiving feedback on the reality of this duration. You become a better judge of time and more aware and confident of your ability to complete tasks in a given period. This reinforces your own trust in yourself, boosts self-confidence and also allows others to have a greater trust in you because you become someone who does what they say.

When you stick to the schedule for several weeks, there will be a tipping point at which the pain and newness of the process is replaced by the euphoria of being a task-completer. You will get to see that if a task is on the schedule... it gets done.

"..THE BEAUTY OF SCHEDULING IS THAT YOU CHIP AWAY AT THE ESSENTIAL TASKS..."

The more things you put on your schedule... the more things get done. And of course, the more you get done, the more time you have to do things that interest you. It's a win-win situation all the way to a great degree. It's also motivating because the more you do towards your study, the more you want to do.

But it's all too easy to wake up one morning to find the schedule isn't set for that day. The potential is for you to have a lie-in and to stop filling it in. It's easy to neglect the task, especially in the first few weeks. If this happens, all you need to do is print off a copy and start again. Fill it in from that point in time for the rest of the day.

You'll always have lots of tasks to allocate a time, so don't beat yourself up if you miss a day or two, don't get depressed, just start up again and get those tasks completed.

Scheduling is a really difficult thing to get started, especially if it means tackling all those jobs you've been putting off. Also, once you start, the temptation to stop can be really compelling at times. But scheduling is a great behaviour to develop and continued practice makes it easier (and rewarding) as time passes.

In an effort to expose you to as many good habits as possible, for you to be a smarter student, this next chapter introduces you to a few behaviours you might want to consider. The chapter that follows it deals with some you might want to avoid.

CHAPTER 7
HABITS WORTH DEVELOPING

"Successful people are simply those with successful habits."

— Brian Tracy

We all have habits that we've developed over the years and it apparently only takes six weeks to develop a new one. A habit is the repetition of activity and approximately a month and a half later it can become part of daily life.

I guess that if you resist the new habit-forming activity it could take longer and if you can see the benefits to your life it might take less. This chapter looks at a few good habits that are worth adding to your life and, since we are all different, it's worth skimming to see if there is anything in here for you.

You probably intuitively know what's good and bad for you, not just as a student but as a member of society and as a future employee. You will have decided what behaviours are important to you when you clarified your personal values in chapter 4.

But that doesn't always stop us exhibiting bad behaviour or doing things that run counter to our values. For the times when you are in doubt, I want to propose a test you can use on your activities which basically asks: *will doing this activity help or hinder my progress?* The answer will hopefully tell you what you should be doing. To help illustrate the point, let me tell you a story that culminates at the 2000 Olympics in Sydney.

7.1 Will it make the boat go faster?

In the 2000 Australian Olympics, the GB Men's eight rowing team were continually off target in their bid to win a gold medal. Britain really did rule the waves in Olympic rowing prior to this with continual gold medals from Sir Steven Redgrave (over five Olympics) and Sir Matthew Pinsent. They have 24 gold medals between them. But in 2000, the Men's eight rowing team were a fractious and argumentative team outside the training environment. Each member had different values and commitments and, whilst they literally pulled together in the boat, they weren't pulling together mentally.

So with some coaching, they decided that as a team and individually, every decision they made including; eating, sleeping, practice, socialising, and egos in the boat... everything... including conjugal relations with their loved ones... would be preceded by the question **Will doing xxxx make the boat go faster?**

The happy ending is, of course, that the GB Men's eight rowing team won gold in Australia that year. Search out the YouTube clip: they pull away for most of the race and it's a nail-biting close finish at the end.

"[ASK YOURSELF]... WILL DOING THIS ACTIVITY HELP OR HINDER MY PROGRESS?"

The way this applies to you is hopefully obvious. The boat relates to your personal goals. Your goal might be to get a *First* or a better degree than your teachers at school said you would get or better than your previous year's results predict. Or your goal might simply be to have a great time at university and get a good degree; minimum work – maximum fun (though I'd caution against this approach).

Whatever your goal, I want you to start to think about your behaviours relating to; staying in the pub for another pint, staying in bed for another 30 minutes, skipping the xxxx lecture, missing a team meeting, spending another 10 minutes texting, jumping into Facebook again or playing computer games. They could be seen as procrastination and I'd encourage you to ask yourself if doing these things will *make your boat go faster.*

Of course, a more beneficial list would be; get up at 7am instead of 8am, write up yesterday's lecture notes in the one hour gap before the next lecture, extend today's schedule to 11pm. All these items would make your boat go faster.

Stopping doing the schedule or dropping a day from it does not make your boat go faster so don't go there. If you want a day off, write it in, that isn't a problem; if it's on the schedule, you can have a day clear without the nagging guilt that you should be doing something else. Just make sure you aren't skipping your student commitments. After all, each lecture and tutorial missed costs you around £36 per hour.

So let's have a look at some more of these helpful behaviours, in the hope that one or more will strike a chord with you.

7.2 Helpful behaviours

"Good habits, which bring our lower passions and appetites under automatic control, leave our natures free to explore the larger experiences of life. Too many of us divide and dissipate our energies in debating actions which should be taken for granted."
— Ralph W Sockman

You are as you are, but you can change the current you to a better version if you so wish. You don't have to be particularly motivated to do something, you just need to make it a priority, requiring some action.

Reading this book for the first time is likely to be quite a wake-up call, but the more you commit to the advice contained within, the more achievements and satisfaction you will get from your life. The secret is in first identifying bad habits and deciding if you want to do something about them. You should also start to congratulate yourself for the good habits you have. A lot of this is about deep self-reflection… difficult to do if you haven't done so before.

So let's just think for a moment about some of the icons we might consider emulating, people who have done well for themselves; business people, world leaders and self-sacrificers. Consider now whether they got to their position in life with a preponderance of good or bad habits.

People like: Sir Richard Branson, Angela Merkel, Prof. Steven Hawking, Mother Theresa, Marie Curie, Steve Jobs and Nelson Mandela would have developed a diverse and generally positive set of helpful behaviours to enable their high workload, productivity and success in their chosen field. We can learn a lot from these characters on our journey to grow more productive and to be happy with our life.

So, I recommend putting 30 minutes into today's / tomorrow's schedule to investigate the electronic presence of a living hero. See if they have a personal website and track down any Facebook, Twitter, LinkedIn, Instagram or YouTube profiles and get a feel for their level of personality and wisdom. Some people in the public eye, who many would consider worth emulating, develop strong altruistic tendencies and are happy to spread their wisdom digitally.

Often referred to as **Thought Leaders**, their wisdom is all there for you if you are prepared to read. Richard Branson (Virgin), for example, is quite active on LinkedIn. Bill Gates (Microsoft) heads and funds the Gates Foundation which strives to bring better health to many of the less fortunate parts of the world. The TED Talks, with their **Ideas Worth Spreading** mantra, provide thousands of inspirational and educational video presentations given by the world's most eminent specialists, industry leaders and prominent creators.

This exercise is about finding some worthwhile characteristics of a hero / heroine of yours that you can emulate and benefit from. Even if they are a popular comedian or singer, you will likely discover that they have an amazing work-ethic and a can-do attitude.

You can glean a lot from these heroes and heroines; take a look in your university library for their autobiography and put time into your schedule to read it. Not there? Try your town library or the many charity shops in your local town / city that all seem to have second-hand books for sale. For anyone remotely connected with computers, technology and music, a must-read is the Steve Jobs official autobiography. Modern history and politics, then the autobiographies of two BBC reporters: Frank Gardner and John Simpson are must-reads.

So here are some good habits that you may consider adopting, categorised by health, wellbeing, studentship and social.

7.3 Maintaining your Health

"It is health that is real wealth and not pieces of gold and silver."

— *Mahatma Gandhi*

7.3.1 Exercise and Fitness Habits

Early morning exercise, before breakfast or washing is good for you. Try a number of sit-ups, push-ups, star jumps, squats, whatever... something to get your cardio-vascular system pumping and metabolism kick-started. Start small and increase the number you do as you get fitter.

Get off your bus a stop early and walk further to your destination. If driving, don't pay to park close, instead park farther away in a free area (save some money) and walk to uni. Take the stairs instead of the lift.

For every 30 minutes of sitting at your desk or at your computer, stand up and do 5 minutes of gentle stretching and movement – get the blood flowing. Take a walk every day, not just to the bus stop, but around the block, or further afield, just for the sake of it. Take in the views and fill your lungs with fresh air.

If you need help and support to start running, find a buddy and have a jog or a run every other day. Start slowly at first, building up to running. Sports clubs at uni (football, rugby, running, cycling volleyball, hiking etc.) provide great exercise and help with socialising and networking. Be attentive to how you feel while exercising, pushing yourself to the point where it's challenging, yet not unpleasing. You will be able to do more as the weeks pass.

7.3.2 Healthy Eating and Drinking Habits

"One cannot think well, love well, sleep well, if one has not dined well."

— *Virginia Woolf*

One of the first things you do in a morning is have a pee. To make up for the fluid loss, have a cup of water within 30 minutes. Breakfast should include slow energy-release carbohydrates to stop you feeling hungry and to balance your blood-sugars. A healthy breakfast should include fibre, protein small amounts of fat and complex carbohydrates.

Carry a water bottle when you leave your house and take regular sips throughout the day. Fill as required and know where to top it up on your daily lecture route. Make your own sandwiches to take with you for snacks and lunch, a healthy and cost-effective option to buying ready-to-eat food.

An extra serving of vegetables added to a daily meal is good, as well as substituting less healthy foods (crisps, chips, chocolate) with fruit, vegetables and unsalted nuts. Increasing your intake of dark-green-leaf veg is very good for you (spinach, winter cabbage, kale).

Smaller meals eaten more regularly are good, perhaps mid-morning and mid-afternoon snacks of oatcake biscuits, bananas or nuts will help sustain you. This habit manages hunger, helps reduce over-eating and maintains a healthy weight.

Having a meat-free day (or two) helps to reduce fat intake and bad cholesterol. Substituting lean protein (chicken or fish) for red meat once or twice per week is good too.

Plan your meals a few days in advance and never go food shopping on an empty stomach – you are more likely to buy some high-energy foods containing fats and sugars to compensate. Eat wholemeal bread with grains rather than white and consider substituting sugary puddings with fruit and other wholesome foods.

Eating slowly and more mindfully will increase your enjoyment of the food (and any company) and also gives time for your stomach to send it's *I'm full* messages to the brain.

Reducing your alcohol intake will pay big dividends with your studies: less hang-overs, less dehydration, less brain-addling and more concentration for study. Your mood and general sense of wellbeing will also improve.

Adding a slice or squirt of lime or lemon to hot or cold water will provide vitamin C and make it taste more interesting. I have drunk hot (boiled) water on its own for many years, it's actually quite tasty and very good for the body.

High-content sugar drinks and those containing caffeine should be avoided as a regular drink. They increase the risk of obesity, diabetes and are steadily rotting your teeth. They are addictive and may need a slow steady reduction to kick the habit. Try replacing with herbal teas.

Beware the caramel-type syrups that can be added to coffees; they can contain as much as 20 spoonfuls of sugar in one helping. Avoid caffeine, cream and sugar where possible and use them as a treat if necessary. Caffeine taken after mid-afternoon may cause sleeplessness.

7.3.3 Living longer

"It's not the years in your life that count. It's the life in your years."
— Abraham Lincoln

As George Bernard Shaw said, *"Youth is wasted on the young"*, because (he believed) that the young tend not to fully appreciate their freedoms. You are young, probably feel invincible and so far away from your *twilight years* as to be immortal. So living longer, as a concept, might seem rather perverse... why spoil the fun? However, ask your parents or grandparents; living longer is more about living longer independently, without ailments such as diabetes, Alzheimer's and cancer. So the following really are life-prolonging habits.

Drink green tea two or three times a day. It supposedly helps brain function whilst also helping burn off fat. The antioxidants may lower cancer and Alzheimer's risks whilst protecting teeth from gum disease and infections.

Exercising vigorously for 10 minutes before leaving the house each morning will work wonders for your heart and get oxygenated blood to your brain.

7.3.4 Healthy sleeping

Don't drink alcohol to help you get to sleep; drink a cup of something soothing like herbal tea (no caffeine) an hour before bed. Don't drink too much, you don't want a full bladder waking you up before your alarm clock goes off. Don't drink or eat caffeine food stuffs in the four hours before bed and make sure you aren't subjecting yourself to blue-light from electronic devices in that last hour.

Try to go to sleep the same time each night on a work day; routine is your friend here. Try to wake up at the same time each morning (including Saturday and Sunday.)

Read a novel for at least 15 minutes before you go to sleep (30 minutes or more is better) and, just before sleeping, visualise something pleasant and calming as you start to nod off. Having the bedroom cold with lots of warm duvets / blankets over you is better than trying to sleep in a warm room.

7.4 Emotional Resilience

"We are all serving a life sentence, and good behavior is our only hope for a pardon."
— Douglas Horton

Bad tempered friends, assignment / exam pressures, money troubles, poor health of a family member and many more issues can really upset the mood and study rhythm of students. Having a robust emotional resilience is going to help prevent the see-sawing of mood and lower the risk of depression and other negative spirit-sapping states.

7.4.1 Personal Growth

It is a good idea to read something educational, inspiring, informative, or uplifting to aid self-awareness and inner development.

Read at least one fiction book every two weeks. It's a great leveller and helps broaden the mind; it could be part of your going-to-bed schedule. It is a form of escapism and it helps unlink the activities and worries of the day with the mind-quietening task at hand. Read at least one autobiography every quarter year. They will give you unexpected insights and observations. You may even become more reflective about your own progress and development; something to be encouraged.

"There is nothing noble in being superior to your fellow man; true nobility is being superior to your former self."
— Ernest Hemingway

You need to remind yourself of your goals regularly. One way is to buy an expensive, precious and 'special' notebook and write them up. Alternatively, printing them out on the Goals Sheets (chapter 5) and fix them to your bedroom wall or at the side of your computer is also good. These goals are your personal treasure and should be viewed as often as possible to keep you focused.

Are you making choices in order to please other people before yourself? Reflect on this and why you are doing it and start to make decisions to suit yourself and your values.

Be aware of when you begin to complain and moan. Instead, say something positive and show gratitude. If you hear yourself making excuses or selling yourself as a victim, practice being really honest and take responsibility for your part in past events.

Someone who whinges doesn't have the time or mind-set to be a creator. You should develop a habit of creating opportunities, products, services, blog posts (whatever is in your area of study) rather than floating through life and complaining.

Have a positive mind-set (glass half full), behave compassionately and generously toward everyone you encounter and spend time working on eliminating your limiting beliefs (such as: I'm not clever enough, I'll never get a First etc.). You need to be mindful and aware every time you bring yourself down so you can challenge and turn around these thoughts.

7.4.2 Self-Confidence Habits

"Success is most often achieved by those who don't know that failure is inevitable."
— Coco Chanel

Address issues of body language. Smiling is good and looking people in the eye when talking is an open, confident and socially desirable behaviour. Walk with an air of confidence and don't drag your feet; literally lift your feet when you walk.

When standing, stand up straight, shoulders back, with your hands hanging naturally at your sides is also good. Don't rely on fidgeting when nervous and instead concentrate on the person talking and what they are saying.

Take pride in your personal appearance; dress well, keep your hair smart and to a style; groom yourself well. You feel more self-confident when you look your best.

Be brave each day and be yourself. Don't be led in to being false or voicing falsehoods. Be genuine, helpful and open; be authentic and practice speaking to someone new every day. Being prepared in intimidating situations will help you be more confident and achieve your goals, so prepare your thoughts and words well in advance of any confrontations, if possible.

7.4.3 Personal Habits

"The chains of habit are too weak to be felt until they are too strong to be broken."
— Samuel Johnson

Get in to the habit of getting enough sleep. A few late nights aren't going to hurt you, however regular short sleeps will impact on your immune system, concentration and critical thinking skills. A regular night-time ritual works well for calming the mind before sleep.

Brushing your teeth every morning (after breakfast) and every evening (shortly before bed) will help keep your gums healthy and make your teeth last a lifetime.

Whenever you receive a gift, send a *Thank You* card or, better still, a letter. Stamps are quite costly now, but imagine how you would feel receiving a well-penned thank you from someone you gave a gift to. If you are going to email, make the text memorable and from the heart.

"BE BRAVE EACH DAY AND BE YOURSELF."

Don't spend excessive amounts of time reading, listening or watching the news, unless your degree benefits directly from this knowledge. Keeping abreast of current affairs is important but can be a good excuse for procrastination or cause you to have low mood (most news-worthy TV news is bad)!

Save, save, save. Decide how much money you are going to save each week, put it in a jar and reduce your spend during that week to suit. Drink water instead of lattes or colas, miss out on the shop sandwiches – make your own packed lunches.

Take a mini technology-detox and practice being mindful of your situation and surroundings. Find a quiet corner, turn all your devices off (that means off rather than to vibrate) and chill out. Think of pleasant thoughts (sun, holidays, friends). This is akin to meditation and helps quieten the mind so you can tackle your many tasks with greater efficiency. Ten minutes of quiet in a hectic day can really put you back on top.

Be open to the idea of noticing and observing your own emotions. When you are feeling low, try to work out what caused it and think of something uplifting. Don't beat up on yourself if you do things you don't want to do. Just re-adjust your mood, thoughts and actions, then carry on. During the day, notice how the people around you make you feel — whether they energize and uplift you or drain you.

Be more mindful of the foods you buy, start reading contents labels, especially relating to sugar. Notice how you feel after eating or drinking sugary and caffeine-laden foods.

If you become stressed during the day, take five minutes to work out the source and create a plan to resolve the situation. Many stresses are caused by a lack of information.

When you experience negative emotions (sadness, anxiety, anger, etc.), practice having your *higher self* step outside of the emotions to remind you they are temporary and don't define you.

Create the habit of spending time in nature every day and mindfully appreciating the beauty around you.

Read or watch something that makes you laugh out loud every day. Seek out one or two positive, upbeat people to spend time with every day.

7.4.4 Thinking Habits

"The trouble with having an open mind, of course, is that people will insist on coming along and trying to put things in it."
— Terry Pratchett

Having awareness of your negative thoughts is a powerful way of learning to overcome them. When a negative thought occurs, force yourself to think about something positive. Easier said than done, and it gets easier with practice. Think about a summer holiday, a night out with mates, anything that pleases you. Don't beat yourself up if you find you have been having negative thoughts for hours or days. Just start thinking happy thoughts.

"READ OR WATCH SOMETHING THAT MAKES YOU LAUGH OUT LOUD EVERY DAY."

Gratitude for everything in your life is a very powerful way of being happy and satisfied. Millions of people in the world are so much worse off than you. Taking five minutes a day to consider the things you are grateful for makes you less of an unhappy complainer and a better person to be around.

We always get the same results when we do things the same way, so when starting a difficult task, pause for a moment to work out if there could be a better, more efficient or creative way of getting the task completed.

Smile often, even if you aren't feeling happy. Answering your phone with a smile will achieve a totally different reaction from your caller because they will hear the happiness in your voice. Laughing is good too as it releases feel-good endorphins.

Surround yourself with positive people. Their ways of working and optimism will rub off on you. Find a hobby or past-time that you can feel passionate about and spend at least 30 minutes a day engaged in it. Doing something absorbing is a great stress-buster and mood-leveller.

Take up **mindfulness** as a means of spending less time in your head and more time engaged with the things that are important to you. There are plenty of listen-along mindfulness sessions on the web. Listen to a few in a tranquil safe place and see if you can quieten your mind. It's a great skill for taking the panic out of life at assignment and exam / revision times.

Begin to pay more attention to the details of your life - What sounds can you hear? What different herbs are in that pizza? What can you smell right now? Being more attentive will stop your mind racing and allow greater focus on the tasks at hand.

Give yourself permission to let go of worry and regret. They won't help you now or in the future. You aren't your past so make the best of now.

7.5 Studentship and Career

"What is a master but a master student? And if that's true, then there's a responsibility on you to keep getting better and to explore avenues of your profession."
— Neil Peart

This section is all about being the best student you can be.

7.5.1 Study Habits

Try to attend every lecture, tutorial, seminar, workshop, lab session etc. Email the relevant lecturer in advance of, or soon after, a missed session, giving the reason, and ask if you need to do anything specific about the missed content.

Write-up lecture notes within 24 hours if you can. This also helps with understanding, information retention and retrieval as well as giving you an excellent resource from which to revise.

Make sure all weekly learning from lectures and tutorials is understood. If not, make a note and ask questions of your lecturer in the next session or via email. Complete all weekly tutorial sheets and labs and do not fall behind. Easier said than done, so try and get a study-buddy who you can share notes with and who can help you with missed classes. This is a two-way relationship, one you need to put effort into.

Work extra hard to catch up if you have been ill and consider asking lecturing staff for special consideration if illness lasts a few weeks or more (the teaching staff really need to know these things). Many universities have special dispensation for illness in the form of extensions, approved extended deadlines and phased return to study.

"..BEING EARLY ISN'T A PROBLEM, BEING LATE IS."

Read and understand all assignments on the day of release and schedule work on the assignments thereafter. Ask your lecturer if you do not understand any part of the assignment.

Keep your room neat and tidy at all times if possible. Given the choice, you'd choose a clean and tidy room to sleep in... so take responsibility.

Keep your desk tidy and organised. It's so much more empowering starting work in a clean environment.

Make sure your computer desktop is organised and large files are stored away in the hard drive folders. Lots of large files sitting on your computer's Desktop will make it slow to start up and to run. File that stuff away.

Create and maintain a well-ordered filing system for lecture notes and other paperwork. Make copious copies in multiple cloud drives.

7.5.2 Organisational Habits

"Organising is what you do before you do something, so that when you do it, it is not all mixed up."

— A. A. Milne

Schedule out your entire day, at least a day in advance. Don't wait to do today's schedule today, it should be set before you sleep.

You need to factor in at least fifteen minutes leeway if driving to appointments, 30 mins if using public transport and five minutes if walking. Remember, being early isn't a problem, being late is. And it can easily take 10 minutes or more to find a specific room in a complex building.

Pay bills as they arrive and file away the paper. Don't let it hang around. All the junk post needs recycling and remember to put your black and recycling bins out on the correct days. If in doubt, your Council's website will have the dates for your postcode. Some councils will fine householders for having rubbish on the pavement on wrong days and also if the refuse / recycling split is not as required.

A place for everything and everything in its place. Return things to their places as soon as possible, especially pots, pans and cutlery (they will likely need washing first!). Clutter will anchor your mind to a mess, whilst a clean and tidy environment allows your mind to move on to solving new problems and to being creative.

7.5.3 Productivity Habits

"If you spend too much time thinking about a thing, you'll never get it done."
— Bruce Lee

Really focus on getting your schedule tasks completed. Allocate the most difficult tasks for times when you are most productive. The more mindful you are, the more exciting the game of task-setting and task-completion.

Make sure to take a break every hour to get the blood pumping, stretch your back and legs. Make sure you drink regularly, and don't wait too long to empty your bladder, you can do damage by holding on too long.

Arrive for classes early and make a point of not missing those 9am Monday and 4pm Friday ones. These are the ones that other students miss, thereby giving you a better staff / student ratio.

Sequester yourself for 45 minutes each day where you can apply yourself, uninterrupted, to tasks. Some libraries have rooms you can book for quiet working; consider booking one or putting on noise cancelling earphones and posting a *Do Not Disturb* sign on your bedroom door during this time each day.

Having an eDetox for days or a week can work wonders for concentration. If this sounds fantastical, just set aside an hour each day where your *Do Not Disturb* sign is visible, email and other social accounts are turned off, YouTube and other non-essentials are turned off on your computer. Perhaps turn off Wi-Fi on devices if not required; anything to keep you mindful and focussed.

Notwithstanding the last item, you could use your smartphone to provide a timer facility. Set a timer for 30, 45 or 60 minutes and test yourself to do as much work in those minutes as possible. Keep setting personal bests and don't stop until the timer stops you.

Clear your room and desk of clutter. If you haven't used something for 12 months, it's probably not worth keeping. Bin, recycle, give it away or sell on eBay. Just get rid, it's holding you back.

Get out of bed earlier than normal. Getting up increasingly early gives you more time to be productive. Getting a solid hour of work done before the world wakes up is a magical feeling because it is frequently very productive and lacking in distractions.

7.5.4 Stress Management Habits

"The greatest weapon against stress is our ability to choose one thought over another."
— William James

At assignment and exam time, you will often feel stresses. There are many techniques for handling the demanding voices and self-doubts in your head, but one of the simplest and most effective is, in a quiet room, to quieten the mind by breathing deeply focussing on your breath. As soon as your mind wanders, guide it back gently to the breath flowing in and out of your nose / lungs, and maintain this for at least five minutes. It takes practice and very difficult at the beginning, but well worth the effort.

Stretching your back, limbs and rubbing the scalp are good for getting oxygenated blood flow back to the body which is good for critical thinking and problem solving.

Schedule in some non-study quality time... listen to something calming and distracting, observe a beautiful view, take in the fragrant smells in a garden, sit in the sun with its warmth on your face and just enjoy the calm.

> "TAKING A POWER-NAP IN THE AFTERNOON CAN BE VERY REFRESHING IF YOU ARE WORKING LONG HOURS..."

Spend time on yourself doing personal-care tasks such as filing your nails or shaving. Taking a power-nap in the afternoon can be very refreshing if you are working long hours and plan to work late that day. Don't sleep for too long (20 to 30 minutes should be fine) otherwise you might not feel tired when you finally go to bed.

7.5.5 Business Habits

Spend at least one hour each week building assets towards a portfolio of work. This could be a blog post in your subject area or contributions to forums. Focus on using industry keywords and search for appropriate images with free-use Creative Commons licenses.

If you are in a more creative area such as art, fashion, computing etc. you need to be making lots of assets and bundling them in an industry-appropriate way that can be easily viewed. A YouTube

Channel, WordPress blog, LinkedIn profile are all potential avenues for you to promote yourself and to be discovered by others.

Networking seems an odd occupation for students, but never before have your opportunities to connect and influence others been so great. The combination of meeting senior industry figures at professional-body evening meetings and the follow-up potential of connecting via social media is a chance not to be missed. Companies are looking for graduates and interns who know how to differentiate themselves positively, you need to take a professional approach here.

The best employees are ones who know their business / sector inside out. You can start by subscribing to appropriate and professional blog posts / newsletters / articles and the like. You get a cutting-edge view, get to hear the latest problems and answers and it will help enormously with professional small-talk when networking or in a job interview.

7.5.6 Career Nurturing Habits

"Wanting to be someone else is a waste of the person you are."
— Marilyn Monroe

Spend some serious time furthering your research into the job role(s) you would like to obtain on graduation. This knowledge will help shape your approach and should help to keep up momentum when you are feeling a little unmotivated.

Arrive for lessons early every day. Don't waste those long gaps between timetabled sessions; plan to write up notes, work on assignments, revise for exams. Fill this time appropriately so you have more time for fun activities in the evening - practice the art of being profitably busy.

Avoid unnecessary meetings or interruptions that waste your time. Are your friends being too friendly?

Research and practice making small-talk, attending for interviews and your presentation skills. Find a small group of like-minded students who are willing to join you in such practice.

Rehearse presentations in the mirror beforehand, record them on your smartphone and watch the replay. Learn from the feedback.

7.6 Social Goals

"It's better to hang out with people better than you. Pick out associates whose behavior is better than yours and you'll drift in that direction."
— Warren Buffett

University can be very lonely without friends. You need to make some good ones, and keep them. Friendships are like garden flowers, they need nurturing, feeding, watering and sometimes pruning. You need to be proactive in staying in touch.

Choose a good set of supportive friends who have a similar work ethic and ethos to you. Learn from them; their outlooks, their creative approach to learning, their ambitions etc.

You should listen and be aware when your friends may be struggling and need your input. Friends are a strong normalising force in life and greatly aid our emotional resilience and morale. Take time to plan fun things with them; a group of friends have a wonderful synergy – the whole being more than the sum of the parts.

You should practice being open and honest with friends. You sometimes need someone to listen to, and to share, both good and bad life events.

It's good to show gratitude, so tell your friends how much you appreciate their support. Treat everyone as you would like to be treated. Smile and laugh more, it's a great bonding activity and will make you more popular.

Start to ask open-ended questions in social settings; ones that indicate you don't anticipate a particular answer or show preferences, and work towards establishing common interests.

So, we've had a quick look at what good behaviours you may want to adopt or reinforce. Now it's time to take a look at a few of those little quirks that are less than desirable. You may have some of these idiosyncrasies yourself, or perhaps spot some of them in your friends.

It's always good to get a wider perspective on why certain behaviours are undesirable and what we can do to overcome and avoid them. So I encourage you to be really reflective with the next chapter and think about whether any relate to you.

The next chapter is a spoof, a reversal on the usual method of providing advice. It's written so as to capture your attention relating to all those little things you do (or don't do) that can work against you. It starts by telling you how to fail in your studies. Are you doing anything to sabotage your own efforts? Read on and find out.

CHAPTER 8
HOW TO FAIL YOUR DEGREE

"Most people don't have that willingness to break bad habits. They have a lot of excuses and they talk like victims."
— *Carlos Santana*

Your university life is littered with lots of good advice and recommendations from academic staff informing you how you can excel at your studies. They tend to come from the *Here's how to do better* or *Here's how to solve a problem* directions. Often, you can anticipate the good intentions and advice and thus turn off to them; you've heard it all before. And if you aren't interested, it has no impact.

So here's a different tactic. This chapter is going to tell you how to **excel at failing your studies**. Do everything on the list to *fail miserably*. Of course, it's a tongue-in-cheek approach, to get your attention and make you think of how you currently approach your studies. Are some of your behaviours drawing you away from high grades?

So here it is, the **Big List of How to Fail Your Degree** - a long list of what we might consider as *bad behaviours.* Please don't try these in your degree studies!

8.1 Excel at being a Bad Student

"If at first you don't succeed, give up and try something else."
— Anon

Being really poor at managing your time can be really stressful for some students. But handing in poor quality work is a really good way of having your course tutors chase you. It can be quite interesting to see the lengths they will go to to get hold of you.

Less than 50% attendance? Don't worry. If you get in to trouble, they'll call you in for a polite chat. Remain calm, invent a serious contageous illness and ask for more time on assignment work.

You don't really need to take notes nowadays, especially with all the lecture content uploaded to a Virtual Learning Environment (VLE – Blackboard, Moodle etc.). Who carries pen and paper nowadays, anyway? If it was important, you'd probably record the session on your phone.

Do your work at the last minute - play all term and do your work and exam revision in the last few days. You'll get a second chance to do the work - Referral / Resits, so why bother stressing for a whole term / semester, just have fun instead. Facebook, computer games and alcohol are your stress-busting friends here – use them as much as possible to take away your worries.

Put in plenty of effort and imagination to create lots of really good reasons for handing your work in late or for why the quality of your work is poor. This can pay off big-time when you are doing your refer work and all the equipment and resources for your course are available because everyone else has passed and gone home. You also max out on that special one-to-one time with staff, assuming they aren't on their summer holidays.

Still want lecture notes but can't be bothered to turn up for classes? No worries, cajole a friend to make a copy of theirs for you. Make sure they are conscientious though, good handwriting and detailed notes are essential.

"A friend in need is a pest, so get rid of them."
— *Anon*

Assignment specifications and exam questions are only for guidance. What the lecturers really want is to know how much you know on a topic of your own choosing. Don't worry about grammar and spelling, by the way, they usually know what you are trying to say.

The Internet has everything you need! People only publish text to the web that is completely unbiased and true – completely believable. Your university Library just holds copies of stuffy old books to impress mums and dads, so nothing there for you when Google has it all. And you don't even need to get out of bed to do the surfing. In fact, Google can be a little random, so try Wikipedia where everything has been written by experts who only tell the truth.

Plagiarism. OK, so you need to be really careful here, but, doing it well (i.e. not getting caught) could save you many hours / days / weeks / months of work. A word of caution though: you do need to stay away from this activity where **TurnItin** is being used, but everything else is fair game. Just make sure that, if you get caught, you have a conveniently dated Death Certificate of a loved one to hand. This way, you might still have to do the work again, but you should be able to avoid having to repeat the whole module next year or being thrown off your course.

So, which is worst; arriving for class late or not at all? At least your lecturer doesn't blow a fuse with your lateness if you don't show at all. A Win:Win all round, and it's all on the VLE when you can be bothered to look.

Saying you **left your work at home** is a great excuse to get you out of the negativity of crits and tutorials or to mask your lack of progress from last week. Most lecturers have never heard this one before, so make sure you use it often. Having forgotten your books at home is also another exceptionally good and rarely used excuse when confronted by your lecturer.

Don't worry if you continually snooze-off or zone-out in class. Lots of others will be doing it too, it just means the lecture isn't that interesting or isn't relevant to the assignment / exam and hence not worthy of your attention.

Sitting at the back is great, especially in a large lecture theatre. You can see what everyone else is doing on their phones and tablets, plus you get a chance to rest your eyes and catch up on some sorely needed sleep.

OK, so here's the best academic tip ever. Ready? When you fail any of your exams, assignments, in-class tests etc. make the biggest loudest uproar about how you weren't given enough time, how it wasn't fair, how you have been disadvantaged etc. etc. Make sure you do it in class with plenty of witnesses, the louder the better for getting what you want. You are the customer, after all.

8.2 Bad can be healthy too

"Good and bad men are less than they seem."
— Samuel Taylor Coleridge

Missed your monthly bath? Clothes needed washing a few weeks ago? Stinky breath, armpits or feet? Not a problem! Everyone will be impressed with your dedication to studies despite your obvious and justifiable poverty in not being able to afford soap.

Students can't afford fresh food; and the marketing message that Five-a-day being good for you is an urban myth. Besides, you are still young, invincible and your body can recover from any illness, hangover or strong curry...overnight. Not a problem; eat and drink whatever you want.

You can't party too much as a student. It's what university was invented for. Of course, you will have to show your face in class now and then, but don't let that interfere with Beer O'Clock.

Having lots of fun, but still need to hand some work in or pass a few exams? No worries; you need to pull an all-nighter, or two. Your young body can go days without sleep with the right amount of caffeine. So line up the Red Bulls and work that midnight oil.

After all, a couple of party-free nights isn't much in the scale of things.

Don't worry about exercise. Life is too short to get your heart pounding and getting all hot and sweaty. Perhaps your body doesn't look good in lycra. Not a problem. Exercise is for freaks; besides, it's so nice watching TV or playing computer games.

8.3 Be unorganised and successful

"Always put off what you can do today, it might not be needed tomorrow."
— Anon

There's no point getting up too early, especially if you aren't feeling adequately sober. So just relax in bed, no one will miss you in morning sessions. Have a *Duvet Day*, lots of others are doing the same thing. You wouldn't be able to concentrate in class anyway.

Procrastinating by playing computer games? Don't worry, everyone's doing it. You'll be fine. It's a really good stress-buster. Ignore problems, they are there just to cause you stress. Ignore them and they'll go away.

Facebook and Twitter. There's a reason why billions of people spend hours on these accounts every day. If they can do it, so can you.

Listening to music while you study is a great way of doing two things at the same time. You are that unique multi-tasker that can do both... wow, awesome. Besides, it's not that loud or too distracting for most of the time, so no worries.

Make sure you live in a shared house as soon as possible. The more people the better so that they can share your cleaning and other undesirable duties.

A tidy room is the sign of a sick mind. Make **Clutter is Cosy** your mantra. Indeed, working from home is great because there are so many other multi-tasking opportunities: make a cuppa, chat with a flat-mate, do some laundry (yes, this can be a better option to working on a difficult assignment), Facebooking your next party. etc. Just stay away from the Library because it's way too quiet to work in there.

8.4 Summary – back to normality

"If you live long enough, you'll make mistakes. But if you learn from them, you'll be a better person. It's how you handle adversity, not how it affects you. The main thing is never quit, never quit, never quit."

— William J. Clinton

We all get in to bad habits for a variety of reasons; time pressures (especially when close to deadlines), avoidance of discomfort, procrastination, poor diet, lack of exercise. We are human – we prefer the easy options and like taking short cuts. However it is worth considering *self-care* as a foundation and support for self-development.

Think about how different your life would be if you were constantly tired, hungry, hung-over, physically unwell and being a bad student. It's not difficult to understand; take care of the basics before attempting the higher-order development work.

It takes only a few weeks to develop new habits, so start today. Don't look to change several difficult traits at the same time, just choose the one that reaches out to you. Sometimes, one job at a time is quite enough, especially with a busy academic schedule. Don't set yourself up for a fall by giving yourself impossible targets.

You have hopefully had a chance to reflect on how you behave in different situations. Being human is to err, so don't beat yourself up over a few mishaps. Learning from your experiences is a powerful life skill, so be alert to give yourself the space to both reflect on the changes and to make any necessary alterations the next time you meet that situation.

Getting smart with time and technology are two very important areas; harnessing every minute for your benefit as well as using technology to make tasks easier. In the next chapter we take a look at the technology you can use to navigate your many goals, making your life easier and more productive. It is the last chapter before the summary and consider this whilst reading it; you only need to make one of the tools, techniques or apps work for you, for the cost of this book to be repaid many times over.

CHAPTER 9
TECHNOLOGY

"It is exhausting knowing that most of the time the phone rings, most of the time there's an email, most of the time there's a letter, someone wants something of you."
— Stephen Fry

This chapter deals largely with modern technology and its pervasive and consuming effect on modern lives. The aim being to harness the power of software and mobile devices rather than being controlled and distracted by them.

Using technology strategies that work for you whilst studying will certainly help you attain some good results. A reassessment of the way you can utilise some technologies whilst reining back on others will let you achieve far greater results; it's a **smart** approach and I hope that you will give some of the suggestions a try. Here goes...

There are some remarkable pieces of equipment and applications for mobiles and tablets as well as free access to enormous amounts of information and knowledge on the internet. Modern communication devices and associated technology can be a double-edged sword for you as you pursue your academic career.

The good news is that they put the world of information and connectivity at your fingertips; the bad news is that they provide that world of information and connectivity... 24 hours a day. The smart student knows when to use the technology and when to, literally, switch off. So, working smart rather than hard, here are a few things you might consider to include in your repertoire of good and professional behaviours.

9.1 Get smart with your Smartphone

*"It's just madness. First email. Then instant message.
Then MySpace. Then Facebook. Then LinkedIn.
Then Twitter. It's not enough anymore to 'Just do it.'
Now we have to tell everyone we are doing it,
when we are doing it, where we are doing it and
why we are doing it."*
— Mark McKinnon

In the last decade there has been a remarkable evolution in the power and functionality of mobile phones and tablets. A few years ago, the typical smartphone had more processing power than the computer sitting in the Apollo space capsule. But here's the thing; you probably don't appreciate that you are possibly addicted, or certainly controlled by your phone / device and you'd be lost without it. It likely has your messages, photos, videos, contacts, phone numbers and provides your linkage to the outside world. You might be doing your banking and paying bills with it.

Many households don't have a landline, they rely on their mobile phone and broadband connection, especially as 4G has been rolled out across the country and many phone contracts include unlimited downloads. You probably reach for your mobile as soon as it beeps, rings or vibrates to see who has communicated with you and what they have had to say.

Have you watched the people passing by on a typical town street at lunch-time recently? Many walk around, heads down, reading and typing on their mobiles. One state in the America is looking at banning pedestrians who are walking and texting (*petextrians*) on the pavements, oblivious to the dangers and accidents already incurred. Antwerp (Belgium) is addressing the problem by introducing Text Walking lanes so as not to endanger or irritate other pavement users.

Researchers are now starting to observe the different manner in which texting pedestrians walk (**Phone Walk**). It seems that the Inattentional (smartphone) Blindness of texting walkers is impacting on their gait; their subconscious needing to exaggerate the body's movements to provide more stability should they encounter a hazard. Penalties for driving in the UK whilst handling a phone have just been increased after several high-profile cases hit the news.

So the temptation to access your smartphone is great, and in order for you to fully control the time in your day, you need to control it, rather than it control you. The immediacy of the mobile can be very distracting as it draws you in to responding quickly to incoming emails, messages and updates. I recommend that you turn it off or set to silent as default, even the vibrate needs turning off when studying.

Studies have shown that a break in task oriented concentration by a mobile call or text, itself only lasting 15 seconds, can erode the task concentration for up to 15 minutes. You therefore need to lock yourself into a focused cocoon where you will not be disturbed, in order to fully concentrate on your tasks. If you don't, you have to schedule more time to complete the task later, thereby eating away at your leisure time. A half hour or an hour spent going through texts and emails towards the end of the day may be difficult to achieve, but well worth the effort in terms of increased productivity earlier on.

Syncing Email and Contacts with your phone is great, it can be done manually, automatically, only when in a Wi-Fi hotspot – you have the control. I encourage you to turn off the audible tone, so you are not constantly wondering who wants what. The continual sync *pings* of incoming email, text, LinkedIn, Ebay, Twitter, Facebook or any other update can be frequent, persistent and with unpredictable timing. You might not read the update message immediately, but you'll be wondering who or where it originated from, reducing your concentration.

When you respond quickly to direct personal messages, your friends will start to believe that they are having a **conversation** with you and it's easy to get embroiled in a ping-pong of messages. Slow it all down… nothing is that urgent unless you are **expecting** something that urgent.

Your friends will soon get used to not getting an instant reply to their contact. They will take some training. But they will come to respect you for your dedication and concentration. They may even secretly hope that they could be as strong-willed and focused as you.

For best efficiency, you should make a hit-list of all the people you need to call and text and then undertake these in one block of time, as per your schedule, otherwise the focus on your task will be less than 100%. This is the reason why your hourly rate multiplier is set at 4 and not 1.

> ## "A MOBILE CALL OR TEXT, ITSELF LASTING 15 SECONDS, CAN ERODE... TASK CONCENTRATION FOR UP TO 15 MINUTES."

There are apps for managing the way in which phones and tablets give their normal feedback during quiet study periods; we cover these a little in section 9.6 in this chapter.

One advantage of the smartphone is the versatility and speed at which many communication tasks can be achieved, however this can also be its downfall. In recent years a member of the Swedish Parliament posted a picture of his Liverpool Football Club tattoo to his Instagram account. The only problem was that he didn't check the photo (maybe he did); but certain parts of his anatomy were visible on the posted picture. There was embarrassment all round and some interesting publicity on social media. It's probably done his street-cred lots of good, however the moral of the story is **Send in haste, repent at leisure**.

Watch out for any nagging doubts with the **Send** button. If in doubt, go back and check. Warning: never Send (or worse still with a **Reply All**) when angry or feeling vengeful. It's never pretty and it can back-fire with disastrous consequences. Count to ten... slowly. If in doubt, save to your Draft folder and reconsider in the morning.

9.2 Unexpected Gaps in your Schedule

With the best will in the world, you will occasionally find yourself stranded; in your car in a breakdown or queue; in a bus breakdown or queue; stuck on a train in a tunnel; or waiting for your meeting because you arrived early. There are lots of reasons for you to find yourself with spare time which was not necessarily your fault.

> "SEND IN HASTE, REPENT IN LEISURE."

As a smart student, it's a good idea to have something useful to occupy your time while you wait it out. What better than to use your smartphone (or other device) to help you learn, keep you entertained and amused at the same time.

It's natural to try and fill our brains with information when waiting for others and when confronted by a lack of stimulus. So why not do something study-related and constructive with this unexpected free time. I recommend catching up on emails, texts or listening to an interesting podcast... whatever you are able to do that comes later in the schedule. If you resort to the reward of playing a computer game in this time, without doing the work required in your schedule, then you start to cheat your own system. If you are in your car you do need to obey the current regulations regarding use of mobiles, of course.

Podcasts are an under-used and under-valued method for filling spare time. You should consider scheduling in a weekly slot to visit a few useful websites and download some content. As a public service broadcaster, the BBC cannot be beaten on quality and variety. However, there are lot more channels available, so let's get a taste of what's out there:

The **BBC iPlayer** for iOS and Android - clips and shows from all TV UK terrestrial channels (http://www.bbc.co.uk/iplayer)

iPlayer Radio for iOS and Android - nine UK national radio stations with many regional stations. Radio 4 is a haven for deep and well-researched content. Categorised content includes: arts culture and the media, crime and justice, history, money, politics, science and nature (http://www.bbc.co.uk/iplayer/radio)

BBC News app — iOS and Android including business, science, environment, politics, education, music, technology and more. Recently updated and bristling with content.

The **BBC podcasts and downloads page** contains a huge amount of material. Think up a search in your subject area and see what is available. Radio 4 programmes usually mention national and international researchers and universities, thereby giving you additional information for researching a project (http://www.bbc.co.uk/podcasts)

Other broadcasters such as CNN (News & Politics, Business, TV, Entertainment and Specials), Discovery Channel and others provide lots of informative and useful media content. **The Podcast Gallery** (podgallery.org) categorises podcasts; TED Radio, General Tech, Food, Media, Business, Kids & Family, History, Music, English Language and many more. You can listen direct, download or upload a podcast to Google Drive or Dropbox. Try some of these out for your subject and see what gems you can uncover.

Apple's iTunes Library for podcasts is spectacularly good for finding interesting material. There are hundreds of thousands of podcasts in their database, with sectionalised content including... Arts, Business, Comedy, Education, Games, Government, Health, Family, Music, News & Politics, Religion, Science & Medicine, Society, Sports, TV & Film and Technology (https://www.apple.com/uk/itunes).

Apple's iTunes U The iTunes University area is full of educational content both for general consumption via the iTunes interface but also for use in class by teachers and students via iPads. There is a great wealth of materials in here, much uploaded by universities. The UK Open University itself has over 130 courses on iTunes U. Educational categories include: Health & Medicine, Business, Engineering, Teaching & Learning, Science, Psychology and Social Science, Art & Architecture, Literature, Mathematics, Languages, History, Communication & Media, Philosophy, Law & Politics. Generally something for everyone.

There are plenty of apps for iOS and Android to find, store and play podcasts. Search the respective stores for *podcast aggregator app* to find some. The appcrawlr website, (appcrawlr.com), provides a fairly good range of iOS and Android apps for this and other categories of use, other specialised app sites are available.

9.3 Wireless, Bluetooth and Battery

"New security loopholes are constantly popping up because of wireless networking. The cat-and-mouse game between hackers and system administrators is still in full swing."

— Kevin Mitnick

Let's have a look at the prominent phone / tablet features to make sure you get the most from your device. Wi-Fi isn't just for mobiles and tablets. There's a large number of Wi-Fi enabled devices such as the later iPods, (some of which have front and rear facing cameras) and gaming consoles. So you could quite easily have a FaceTime (Apple iOS) or video Skype (Microsoft) chat with a friend or family member whilst in town... from your mp3 music player... using free Wi-Fi.

9.3.1 Wireless Hotspots

Access to thousands of free Wi-Fi hotspots, plus increasing capacity from providers wanting to tempt you to their relatively expensive 4G offerings, have opened up the world of computing on the move. At the moment, many food retailers, supermarkets and café chains provide free Wi-Fi though you may have to make a purchase and usage may be for a limited amount of time.

You may or may not need free Wi-Fi, based on your current provider speed and contract allowance, but waiting for a good hotspot to download a large video or audio (podcast) file is always helpful. The disadvantage is that you may be required to subscribe to that company's email list, although a simple Unsubscribe is all that's required once they become a nuisance.

Service provider O2 (now part of Telefonica) have many hotspots around the country and you need not be their customer. Just register, there are no usernames or passwords and all content is filtered to be safe. Outlets include many of the big chains: McDonalds, Debenhams, Costa Coffee and House of Fraser. You can download the iOS or Android app which can detect and automatically connect. Why not set yourself a challenge in your local town/city to see where they are. Can you walk across town without losing a connection?

Figure 5 shows that there are many such hotspots in Leeds (within 1 mile radius) via the **O2 Wifi Hotspot Locator** (www.o2wifi.co.uk)

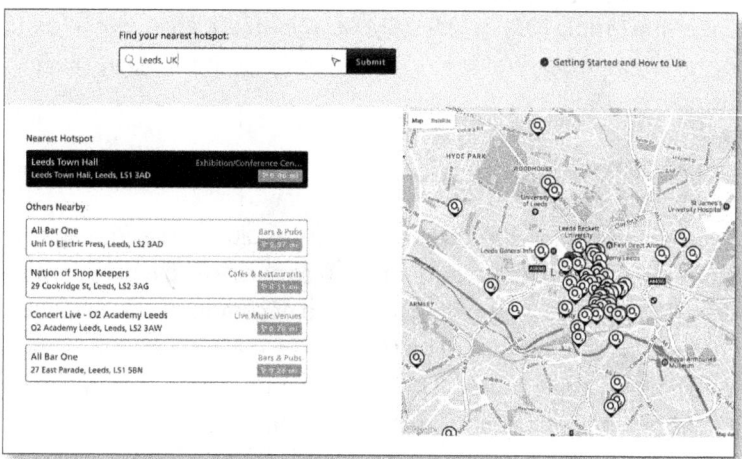

Figure 5 *'O2 Hotspot Locator' showing locations in Leeds*

BT (British Telecom) advertise that they have over five million free Wi-Fi hotspots around the UK and these are piggy-backed from private and business Wi-Fi sources, all BT-based (Figure 6, showing Leeds City centre). You need to be a BT broadband customer, or have a family member who is, in order to allow registration. They also have seven million more spread around 100 countries.

There is a wide coverage of location types including: coffee shops, shopping centres, pubs, bars, train and tram stations, airports, general city centre coverage and homes. The BT Wi-Fi spread is so wide because, by default, every BT customer has 0.5 MB/s reserved from their broadband capacity to act as a free service. Their tie-up with Fon, a Wi-Fi provider, allows other BT Fon enabled customers to access this spare capacity, literally, from the street.

BT Wi-Fi coverage seems to be far more comprehensive than O2. **Figure 6** shows a map of Leeds city centre with specific Wi-Fi sources. The search for Leeds on **BT Wi-Fi finder** also shows a heat-map for areas of high or low connectivity. It's well worth seeing who you know that has BT broadband so that you can be added to their account. Have a look at the BT Wi-Fi finder to see what's available in your area (www.btwifi.com/find/).

Money Saving Tip: Many mobile accounts allow you to increase or decrease your spend and service provision at will. You can probably save £5 to £10 per month by reducing your contract spend and using these free providers. That could be over £100 per year! But beware, some providers will want to lock you in to another 12 months (or more) contract for the privilege.

Figure 6 *'BT Wi-Fi Hotspot Finder' data for Leeds*

9.3.2 Bluetooth

You may have connected devices or transfer content between phone and another device using Bluetooth. The technology is great for ear-pieces and connecting to the radio in modern and high-spec cars. They are great for transferring digital assets from one device to another.

However, this form of (relatively open) access leaves the phone vulnerable to malicious attack and drains the battery. If you use Bluetooth, make sure you turn it off when finished. Some systems have default periods where it closes automatically after use. Be aware that whilst travelling on public transport or navigating a busy city, there will be people looking out to discover any Bluetooth active devices passing by to see what they can *sniff out*.

Bluetooth is also a feature on many older feature phones, rather than the newer smartphones. Since it is a standard embedded communication system, it is generally a lot easier to use than finding and logging on to a Wi-Fi connection, although the process of pairing can be troublesome. And, similar to Wi-Fi, the pairing only needs to happen once for it to be remembered.

"[BLUETOOTH]... LEAVES THE PHONE VULNERABLE TO MALICIOUS ATTACK AND DRAINS THE BATTERY."

One of the great uses of Bluetooth is when you aren't in a Wi-Fi hotspot. You can tether your laptop or tablet to your mobile and use its 3G or 4G signal to provide internet access. But beware, connecting your phone over Wi-Fi will drain your battery faster than a Bluetooth tether. So make sure to turn it off when not in use.

Seek out your smartphone's connection details which shows the status for GPS, WiFi, Bluetooth, Airplane mode and other connectivity options. It allows you to instantly see the status of each feature and turn them on or off. I sometimes forget to turn off GPS Location when using the Maps app and this widget shows if it's still turned on. Leaving it turned on also tells the map provider exactly where your phone is at all times

9.3.3 Battery

The more you use the connectivity to 'consume data', the quicker your battery fades. Using GPS location is a huge drain as is Wi-Fi. Many apps will still be running in the background even after you cancel or change app, so I recommend installing an **App Killer** that sits on the front screen; one touch and every running app is forcibly stopped. They are good for keeping data usage low too.

There are plenty of battery management apps available; these can tell you which applications are using the most power and help you control their use. With mobile screens becoming ever larger and with resolutions more fine, screen display is one of the biggest culprits on battery power. Do you need the display so bright when indoors? If not, turn it down and save power.

Battery power does however need to keep pace with increasing screen resolution as we surpass 550 pixels per inch (Apple's iPhone Retina Display is a mere 326 ppi). Samsung are looking at 2K TV screen resolution which is in the region of 800 ppi. Perhaps we are going back to the age of brick-sized mobiles, where much of the volume is battery.

9.3.4 Data Usage

"Experts often possess more data than judgment."
— Colin Powell

It is useful to review your data usage every few weeks. If your phone allows you to set data alarms (warn you when you get to your inclusive contractual data limit), then you should do so. If you have an unlimited data contract then don't worry. If you are limited however, it can be quite expensive exceeding the limit. Operators can quite readily charge an additional 20% of your monthly contract sum if you go over your limit by a single kilobyte.

There are many data-related apps available, Android phones tend to show actual usage against warning and limit lines set by the service provider (Settings > Data Usage). This area also shows what apps are using the most data. With Apple's iPhone, have a look at **Cellular Data Usage** in **Settings** to get at this information.

If you are on a data-limited contract, always make sure you are on a Wi-Fi network before viewing any videos, though the current rollout of 4G will make this advice redundant in a few years when the country is covered in superfast connectivity and data allowances have grown.

Many service providers offer tiered data packages. Make sure you aren't consistently paying for a high level of data usage when you only use a little. Also consider engaging in daily / weekly / monthly roaming top-ups when going abroad. Vodafone have a £3/day maximum (all calls, all texts and limited data) when travelling around Europe, so be aware of your provider's offerings when abroad. Again, beware reducing your contract allowance as some providers want to bind you to a new one- to two-year contract.

Other data-minimising tips include:

- *Do your downloading when you are on a (fast) Wi-Fi connection. Let someone else pay for all that traffic*
- *Turn off data-roaming when abroad (unless you have a firm handle on what you are using / paying). This can cause huge bills on your return*
- *Set your phone to detect and connect to Wi-Fi when it sees a network it knows*
- *Unsent emails, SMS texts and MMS messages can sit in their respective out-boxes, in an attempt at being continually sent using up valuable data... and battery power. Delete or stop sending where appropriate, especially when large attachments are included*
- *Streaming high quality music or video can use up 100MB to 1GB per hour respectively*
- *Many websites now have a stripped-down mobile version which is more device-friendly. Sometimes their web address is preceded by an 'm', whilst many others serve up mobile-friendly content when accessed by a device. These versions are worth bookmarking as they are more responsive, use less battery power, use less data and are often easier to navigate via the small screen*
- *Clear out the apps you don't use. You'd be surprised just how much memory, cached data and battery power some apps use whilst not in use. Some are constantly returning data on your location, searching for Wi-Fi, Bluetooth and Near Field Communication (NFC). Apps can be forced to stop or be uninstalled*

- Video, audio and picture services such as Flickr and Pinterest use up a lot of data. Use Wi-Fi where possible
- Turn off email auto-sync and manually sync when in a Wi-Fi zone... you therefore don't need to worry about those large attachments
- Analyse each of your apps to see what's using location data in the background. This comes from a combination of GPS (if active) and triangulation from your network cell position
- And finally... when you finish using an app, turn it off.
  If you don't, it's still there in the background consuming data and battery power.

As you can see, a smartphone can be a real minefield once you start to look at where data and battery are draining from. If you are on an unlimited data plan (lucky you) then you just need to worry about the battery. Otherwise, you do need to take a regular look at the data and alter course as required.

9.4 Managing Information Sources

"In an information society, education is no mere amenity; it is the prime tool for growing people and profits."
— John Naisbitt

A word of warning about the remainder of this chapter. There follows quite a long list of useful websites and apps that will help you become more efficient in your work. However, once you enter this rapidly changing world, you soon find that the app you have been using for three months needs updating or has been overtaken in popularity by a competitor. By definition, once this book is published, the content is out of date, so I urge you to do your own research... I'll tell you the best websites to do this, although they too will likely become superseded in time. Have fun with it.

9.4.1 Subject Librarian

"A collection of good books, with a soul to it in the shape of a librarian, becomes a vitalized power among the impulses by which the world goes on to improvement."
— Justin Winsor

Prior to the Internet, academic research took place in libraries with things such as books, journals, inter-library loans, microfiche readers and, more recently, CDs and DVDs. Most of these things are still available and, for example the microfiche reader, might still be required to be used in historical research where data hasn't been digitised. But looking at the vast majority of references in student project work today, they usually start with *http://www...*

Modern university libraries have electronic versions of many assets with added subscriptions to electronic book libraries, such as Safari Online and Books24×7, as well as video training resource subscriptions to Lynda.com and others.

They will also have business and marketing reports (e.g. Mintel, J.P.Morgan, Ipsos MORI), Government statistics and specialised research databases. In fact, your library has a wealth of knowledge that will be invaluable to you... if you only knew it was there.

So, make friends with your subject-librarian and see what they have for you! Seriously, unless you spend a lot of time finding your way around your library assets, you likely know less than a tenth of what's in there. If you rely on the Library web interface, you will only get out of it what you ask.

The old computing maxim applies here - *Rubbish in, rubbish out*, or more appropriately, *Limited query, limited answer*. Ask your subject-librarian for help. They just love helping students and are particularly good at helping with keyword search terms and subject-specific databases.

9.4.2 Social Bookmarking

Unfortunately for unsuspecting students, the power of the Internet is also part of its downfall, academically. There is so much information (many billions of interesting web pages), that you are guaranteed to come across great search results including, awesome reports, plum infographics and fabulous statistics. You will find them via your own PC / Mac, some shown to you by friends on their PCs / Macs, you will find some on the university and library computers, even on your mobile / tablet / device. In fact, you'll find lots of great stuff spread over many browsers, many search histories, having used many machines.

Whilst you can save these links to your browser bookmarks, you end up with different sets of bookmarks or no access to bookmarks on other people's machines. You need a strategy for managing these sources and you need it now.

Welcome to Web 2.0 **Social Bookmarking**. Cloud-based crowd-sourced bookmarking sites can provide an answer because your references live in one place only and are accessible by any browser on any computer. Social networking and social sharing in education is extremely powerful; sites such as **delicious.com**, **diigo.com**, **digg.com** and **stumbleupon.com** were created for you to save, share and find lots of interesting references, blogs, forums and news articles. They aren't always academically accurate but they are invaluable in providing opinion and frequently contain hidden links to more sanitised and solidly researched data.

The basic idea is that you save your search results into one of these cloud-based sites. You can then access the information from any machine at any time via a browser. By socially sharing, other people are able to see the fruits of your labour and you get to see the links that they found when searching for similar subjects (or tags). This is all about standing on the metaphorical shoulders of giants.

If you are looking for references on: reinforced concrete design methods, the life-cycle of the Hairy Wood Ant, thrust-bearing design in high-performance engines, or romantic literature of 17th century Italy, you will be able to see what sources other people have found, in addition to those you discover and save yourself. Search results are all about the keywords you use as input and there are many people out there using different / better search terms than you. Use their results.

There are a variety of differently-focused sharing platforms on the web. You will be familiar with YouTube for video sharing, perhaps SoundCloud for audio, Flickr and Instagram for photos, Twitter for short messages etc., but there are some additional platforms that are particularly good for your student activities.

One way of getting your own search / blog / forum seen by visitors is to register it with one of the many focussed sharing platforms. So it follows that these sites are a good source to find blogs and the like. Here's a few that may be of interest and, as always with the web, there will be many more out there for you to find:

- **Bookmarks.** *delicious.com* and *diigo.com* are the basic competitors in providing cloud storage of your bookmarks. You get to write notes and easily remembered tags for each source saved so that you can find it later. You can also search the tags that others provided to see what they found. This way, you get to harness the search-hours and discoveries of students and researchers before you, much of which has emanated from different search-keywords, hence you can get some spectacular results.

- **Blogs.** Topic experts can give freely and wisely on blogs, but you need to sift through the many thousands available to ensure you aren't reading content from an unwise non-expert. Of the blog aggregators available, **alltop.com** is perhaps the premiere, though **blogarama.com** is up there too and there are many others (Search: blog aggregator). Many have topic groupings and excellent search facilities. Some have Most Popular, Most Recent and other popular viewing criteria. Sites such as: **blogcatalog.com, bloggernity.com, blog-search.com** and **yourversion.com** are all worth a look to see if you can find a useful blog site in your subject area. The latter allows you to find not only blogs, but videos, products, news and Twitter feeds, plus it allows for bookmarking, sharing and even importing of bookmarks from *delicious.com*.

- **Forums and Discussion Boards.** Many search engines allow you to search for forums or boards by simply adding **forum** or **discussion board** after your topic. Alternatively, there are specific forum aggregators that search only forums (boards). Sites such as: **theforumfinder.org, findaforum.net** are useful. Keywords for search include: forum, board, discussion board and message board.

- **Search modifiers.** If you own a blog or forum, you may submit its details to aggregator sites. They provide a search engine friendly way of getting your site seen before your competitors. A few are mentioned above, however if you want to control directly your searches, you can use search modifiers. The two most useful are **site:** and **inurl:**. If you want to search, say, just the bbc website for geology, your search might be **geology site:bbc.co.uk**. If you wanted to find any site relating to geology which had a forum, you might use the inurl modifier, thus: **geology inurl:forum**.

9.5 Type less, talk more

"Any sufficiently advanced technology is indistinguishable from magic."
— Arthur C Clarke

We've already discussed the potential for technological devices to be a distraction from keeping to your schedule. But the technology I want to introduce here could not only save you serious time if used correctly, but expand your horizons greatly.

Every so often I get a student who can touch-type, or I chat with a secretary who is typing whilst talking to me, having sent the email about our discussion to the recipient, without any need to check for errors... or any loss of eye contact. It's very impressive and doesn't happen too often.

The speed and fluency at which thought can be expressed in typed words is an enviable skill in others and one which is already freely available to us in a different form.

If you don't want to learn to touch-type, you can use something like the Nuance *Dragon Dictate* software. It is a simple download purchase from the web, typically with a 50% student discount when verified with an academic email address. I bought a copy for around £50, it came boxed in the post with a microphone headset and is remarkably accurate 'out-of-the-box'. You need to train it to your voice and the mic set-up you will use, but you can quite quickly begin to dictate long lines of text with great accuracy.

Dictation is quite a difficult skill to master; thinking and voicing your text on the fly. Standing up rather than sitting down gives better results, I find. I'm using an extension of the aforementioned technology as I *write* this text. I wrote the majority of this book long-hand on paper, whilst on holiday. But I've used my mobile phone to record myself speaking the text. I then pass narrated mp3 files to **Dragon Dictate** for it to process into text.

There are other systems available, and for free. The current Windows Operating System which comes with voice recognition capabilities (Windows Speech Recognition), actually works quite well out-of-the-box too. It does of course need some voice recognition training to be useful. To do this, you record yourself reading a book or some poetry and it does the rest.

The more you train any recognition system, the fewer mistakes it makes. If you have a Windows PC, have a look in the Search area for *Speech Recognition* and you will get commands to set up your microphone, control the computer without a mouse and start speech recognition. It's all there... who knew?

Apple iOS systems have a dictation facility which until recently needed an internet connection to work. It is similar to the Siri system on iPhones. However, with a large download (over 750MB), the *Dictation* application can work self-contained without internet.

Some independent reports indicate that the inbuilt microphones in a MacBook Pro are good enough without the need for a headset. Again, if you have a relatively recent MacBook, search for the *Dictation* software and see where it leads.

Whilst you may have a desk-based microphone, I do recommend getting a headset mic so that it stays equidistant from your mouth when you move (MacBook comment above excepted). Voice recognition systems are very sensitive to mic position and also to changes between mic systems for your recorded voice profile (jack plugs vs. USB microphones, a case in point).

Some will require you to do separate voice training for each mic setup. My mobile voice recording app required me to record the pre-reading training and have it processed before it knew what to do with my actual voice files.

I recommend you spend a few hours playing with whatever free version you can get hold of, do some voice training (it's worth it) and see if it is something you could use in your studies. Definitely worth a try and, if it works for you, the cost of this book will be repaid many times over on just this one discovery as a result of your enhanced productivity.

9.6 Apps for Smart Working

"Where past generations had film, cameras, scrapbooks, notebooks, and that part of the brain which stores memories, we now have a smartphone app for every conceivable recording need."

— Graydon Carter

Using your smartphone in class is becoming increasingly seen as a legitimate use, due to the proliferation of digital recording, note-taking and research apps available. Many students use their device to record lectures, take pictures of whiteboard content, make notes, save to cloud storage, search for answers to questions (rather than asking in class) and for collaborative class-work. There follows therefore a brief list of apps that may be useful and worthy of your investigation.

Apps live in a very fast-changing environment and anything mentioned in print today, may be updated or deleted by the time you read this. There is a proliferation of apps on a single topic, some good and some less useful; there are over 90 lecture-recording apps available. So which do you go for? The answer is to do a reasonable amount of research; look at download numbers, ratings, reviews, forum comments, Facebook recommendations etc. especially when paying your hard-earned cash.

The following apps are useful and (largely) free at the time of writing, though some are paid apps.

Key: **£0** is free, **<£5** is less than £5 and **<£10** is less than £10. The applications work on any device unless stated otherwise.

Lecture, tutorial and writing aids

- *SoundNote – iOS, lecture capture for iPad, notepad, sketchpad, audio. Store lecture in audio-visual form. <£5*

- *LectureMonkey – iOS, record lectures, take notes. £0*

- *Notes Plus – iOS, another notes and audio lecture capture app, handwriting recognition. <£5*

- *Audio Memos – iOS, lecture audio capture, notes and share. £0*

- *Evernote – digital notebook, scheduler and to-do list. Any device, sync to cloud. £0*

- *Super Notes Recorder – iOS, save and collate notes, recordings, image, alerts, very interactive. £0*

- *FetchNotes – hashtag your notes, the app arranges them for you. £0*

- *Google Keep – Android, add notes, images, audio and lists as they occur. £0*

- *RefME – use for getting formal references from books and other sources. Works with EndNote, Mendeley, Word and others. £0*

- *EasyBib – also creates easy referencing and citing of sources. £0 with ads or <£5 without ads*

- *Prezi – a drag and drop, zoom and pan presentation software to blow the socks off PowerPoint. £0 Edu Enjoy plan*

- *Vocabology – iOS, enhance your vocabulary, even in different languages (beware US vs UK spellings). <£5*

- *Dictionary.com Mobile – a mobile dictionary, voice activation, word-of-the-day. £0*

- *Simplemind+ - visualise ideas with this mind map app, hyperlink and share. £0*

- *Grammar Up – search for, and test, your grammar knowledge. <£5*

- *Quizlet – iOS and Android, quiz yourself on (almost) any subject. £0*

Productivity aids

- *Study Buddy – get efficiency reports on work vs distraction time, plus inspirational quotes. £0*

- *Timeful – iOS, scheduler and time-keeper. Recently bought by Google, so watch this space. £0*

- *Wunderlist – make to-do lists, reminders, notes, share and collaborate. £0*

- *Focus Booster – breaks your time up in to segments for revision and assignment work, keeping you (you guessed it) focused. £0 but limited unless you pay yearly fee.*

- *30/30 – iOS, productivity app for getting tasks done. Work hard for 30 mins, take a break for 30. £0*

- *Remember The Milk – time management tool, scheduler, reminders, to-do lists. £0*

- *iStudiez Lite – iOS, to-do lists, track upcoming assignments, exams and grades. £0 and <£10 for Pro version*

- *Todo – iOS, another list making, task manager, day viewer. <£5*

- *2Do – iOS, task list manager with colour coding, projects, tags, notifications. <£10*

- *Finish – iOS, a to-do list app for procrastinators, it focuses on the reward messages when you complete a job, makes jobs more urgent as time passes by. £0*

- *Listastic – iOS, good and easy to use to-do list tracker. <£5*

- *Trello – visual card-sorting to-do list app. Make check-lists, attach files and pictures, share, collaborate. £0*

- *Timetable – Android, timetable mapper, mute during class, £0*

- *My Class Schedule – Android, class schedules, exam timetables and homework reminder, £0*

- *Class Timetable – iOS, class scheduler and event manager, £0.*

- *Self Control for Study – Android, blocks out social and other apps for a set period to let you study. £0*

Revision Apps

- *Exam Time – (web-based), revision charts, flash cards, mind maps, quizzes and notes. £0*

- *Exam Countdown – iOS, tracks number of days to your exams. £0*

- *StudyBlue – subject-related flash cards and make your own. £0*

Sleeping Aids

- *Alarmy (Sleep If U Can) – wakes even the most stubborn sleepyhead. <£5*

- *Sleep Cycle alarm clock – iOS, wakes you in the optimum part of your sleep cycle to stop you feeling tired. <£5*

Added learning

- *Duolingo – learn French, German, Spanish and other common languages. £0*

- *Google Translate – Android, translate content in many different languages. £0*

Alcohol

- *Wise Drinking – charts your drinking and makes healthy suggestions, drinking rate, drinks diary. £0*

- *Drunk Mode – tests your ability to think before allowing you access to the Send button. Hides certain contacts and shows you where you've been… whilst drunk. £0*

- *Drinkaware: Track and Calculate Units – monitors alcohol intake. Set up a No Drink Day, compare this week's intake with last week. £0*

This chapter bringsww to an end the main elements of what I think may be useful to you in enhancing your technological engagement with studies. Have a try at some of these apps to see if they can accelerate your studies, or merely just to have more fun, or both.

In researching this chapter, it has been quite a revelation in the websites and applications available at little or no cost to you. Like all technology however, someone is always working on the next update of the next best thing. It's certainly an area to keep an eye on, not only as a student, but also in your imminent professional life outside academia.

So we've come to an end and all that remains is to wrap it all up and say goodbye via chapter 10, the Summary.

CHAPTER 10
SUMMARY

"The sexiest thing in the entire world is being really smart. And being thoughtful and being generous. Everything else is crap. I promise you. It's just crap that people try to sell to you to make you feel like less. So don't buy it. Be smart. Be thoughtful and be generous."
— Ashton Kutcher

Most *How To Study for a Degree* books focus on learning, exams, assignments and the fairly intensive educational theory stuff commonly known as Study Skills. But, until you face up to yourself and reflect on what type of person you would like to become (assuming you want to improve) and what you want to do with your life, then nothing much is going to change.

But what if you aren't motivated with your degree or just aren't interested in a piece of work... does it matter? I would argue that you don't need to be motivated about the work itself. We wouldn't get much work done if we had to feel motivated to do everything we did.

Success comes from knowing that we want to do something, that it's on our goals list, not whether we feel motivated about the task or not.

You may have a great work-ethic and enjoy working long and difficult hours with your studies. There are few things as satisfying as working intensively on something that motivates you. But you can't always get excited about doing all your work, so just getting on with it and accepting that it isn't exciting is the way to go

Looking at your studies, you might find that this is an impossible task... but it isn't. All you need to do is change the way you look at your university life and realise that it's just one step for you in achieving what you want.

You probably know someone who aces all their tests, assignments and coursework without seeming to work at all. The chances are that they are working **smart** and not wasting time doing or worrying about things that aren't important, such as whether they're motivated or not. Knowing a lot about what you need to do and then doing it in a managed way is the **smart** thing to do. My intention with this book is to open your mind to the limitless possibilities of being strategic in what you do.

Sometimes you will find that you want to do something different from your plan; something which doesn't move you forward. But all you need to do is say to yourself *'It's just a thought'*, and keep on doing what you should be doing.

This book is about getting you into the right frame of mind, starting now. Even if you aren't a 150+ IQ student, you can beat almost anyone to a top degree by persistence, dedication, valuing your time and laser-focusing your efforts with a schedule.

Are you the sort of person who reads books like this and doesn't get involved with the exercises or undertake the suggestions for work and practice? Did you skip the **Life Values** or **Goals Setting** exercises? If you missed any of the practical work, I encourage you to go back and revisit those chapters. They have the power to profoundly change your life for the better.

> *"Nothing in this world can take the place of persistence. Talent will not: nothing is more common than unsuccessful men with talent. Genius will not; unrewarded genius is almost a proverb. Education will not: the world is full of educated derelicts. Persistence and determination alone are omnipotent."*
>
> — Calvin Coolidge

If you are not intending to do the daily schedules because they look like a lot of effort, then let me tell you this. As long as you resist doing the schedules, they will remain enormous work. But as soon as you let them into your daily life, you will start to rise towards the top of your year. Better still, you will get enormous satisfaction, benefit and happiness. Just imagine that; being happy working.

You now have the formula for measuring the value of your time. For UK students it's roughly £36 per hour though you should input your own figures to reassure yourself. This is not to say you can do consultancy work as a student and actually charge people £36 an hour, it's just a figure to keep your mind focused on what is important and what is a waste of your time. Time is your major asset, but it is in limited supply.

You have hopefully seen that **Life Values** are important to you. Living by your values will make for a vital life; doing otherwise can make you unfulfilled. Values are great for making difficult decisions; does doing xxxx support your values or not?

Most of your future career options and relationships can be weighed up against your values. This is an invaluable insight, one which top entrepreneurs and business people use religiously. Large organisations are currently turning towards using **Values Statements** and assessing candidate's personal values as a decider in job interviews. It's a good area to rehearse for your first round of job interviews.

"AS SOON AS YOU LET THEM [SCHEDULES] INTO YOUR DAILY LIFE, YOU WILL BECOME INVINCIBLE AND RISE TOWARDS THE TOP OF YOUR YEAR."

You now have a value on your time and know what is good and bad for you. This is the time to decide where you want to be in, say, five years' time, and set your goals accordingly. We looked at setting your short-, medium- and long-term goals in chapter 5.

You need to make your goals real for you. Don't just have a guess at what you think you want in the future. Your goals are about what you will achieve by a certain time. There are lots of distractions along your future path and they stand between you and your goals. Whenever you come to a crossroads, just ask yourself *'Will doing xxxx make my boat go faster?'* You will get the right answer for you.

The **schedule** is a prime mover in all this. It's a to-do list, calendar and stop-clock rolled in to one. Your efforts to be a better student may come to nought if you don't partition off your time in to bite-sized chunks with set tasks for each session. Try the schedule for two whole weeks, including weekends, and see where it gets you. It may be hard work, but it will move you forward when done well. As long as you put the jobs you don't want to do on the schedule, as well as the good ones, plus some time for fun activities, you will be amazed at how productive and happy you can become.

So you are now psychologically prepared for (almost) any event. It just happens to be studying for a degree. The lessons you've learnt also set you up perfectly for the rest of your life. This book is really about finding where you want to go in life, how you are going to break it into bite-size achievable steps, using strategies for keeping on track and reacting appropriately to feedback.

This way of thinking is eminently suitable for any part of the rest of your professional and home life. This doesn't involve additional work on your part but focuses on how to maximise your existing resources. Remember, it's all about working *smarter*, not necessarily working harder.

- *Working smart will differentiate you from your peers in all your endeavours*
- *Working smart will save you time and money*
- *Working smart will boost your grades and final degree classification*

- Working smart will create more time for the things you want to do— socialising, hobbies, travel etc.
- Working smart will increase your options and opportunities
- Working smart will make your life more satisfying and happy.

I will leave you with three more quotes. I think they sum up what this book is truly about; **empowering** you. I hope that I have given you the tools to start thinking about yourself as a project; a project that can have aims, missions, achievements and success. I wish you well in all your endeavours and encourage you to:

- Treat others as you would want them to treat you
- Realise that you have a lot to learn from everyone around you, and not just about your studies and
- Reflect and question what it really is that you want to do in life... then turn your powers, determination and focus on getting there.

I've had great fun finding all the quotes, from the rich and famous to the reporters and wordsmiths of the last century and beyond. This quote is about vision, ambition and having faith in yourself. It's a transformation I see in many students, from arriving at Freshers to leaving on Graduation day.

"I've learned that fear limits you and your vision. It serves as blinders to what may be just a few steps down the road for you. The journey is valuable, but believing in your talents, your abilities, and your self-worth can empower you to walk down an even brighter path. Transforming fear into freedom - how great is that?"

— Soledad O'Brien

Please watch out for news about the new book releases and feel free to subscribe to the Newsletter on the **MaxYourDegree** *website* for freebies, tips and news. Also feel free to join me via *comments* and the like on various social media and in the blog posts (**www.maxyourdegree.com**).

'Think Smart. Work Smart' is the first in the **MaxYourDegree** *series* of books from **Planet Student**. At the time of first publication, further books in the series are in the pipeline and will be published commencing 2017.

And for the penultimate quote... something special and emotional:

"Our deepest fear is not that we are inadequate. Our deepest fear is that we are powerful beyond measure. It is our light, not our darkness that most frightens us. We ask ourselves, Who am I to be brilliant, gorgeous, talented, fabulous? Actually, who are you not to be?"
— Marianne Williamson

I wish you all the very best in your studies and beyond. I remain humbled by the intellect, honesty and integrity of students as well as being inspired and invigorated by those I meet in the course of my job.

I hope that this book provides some measure of inspiration and insight for you to differentiate yourself and, in doing so, allow you to find a passion in your chosen area of work. My very best wishes for a fabulous future.

Michael

MAX YOUR DEGREE

CHAPTER 11
REFERENCES & INFLUENCES

"You are the sum total of everything you've ever seen, heard, eaten, smelled, been told, forgot – it's all there. Everything influences each of us, and because of that I try to make sure that my experiences are positive."

— Maya Angelou

The majority of this book flowed from my vast memory bank of student, teaching and learning experiences and was drafted within a couple of weeks on a summer holiday. As soon as I started to sectionalise the content and write, I realised just how much I didn't know and how big the gaps were; much research was needed.

I had been reading lots of web and management-related blog articles at the time. Having assimilated the writings from a wide range of authors (professional and otherwise), it became quite easy to put together the missing bits. I didn't want to turn the book into a research-fest, so here are the *major players* in my quest, a task that I have thoroughly enjoyed, not least because it had an obvious purpose and tangible output. I recommend all of them.

Dan Kennedy

The first of these elements came largely from Dan Kennedy's *No B.S. Time Management for Entrepreneurs* book. Dan is a prolific writer and web marketer and makes a lot of money for a lot of people, including himself. He's the guru's guru and it's written in a kick-ass style. It's well worth getting hold of a copy of his book. It's a little dated now, but its messages are timeless:

"No B.S. Time Management for Entrepreneurs: The Ultimate No Holds Barred Kick Butt Take No Prisoners Guide to Time Productivity and Sanity"
— **Dan S Kennedy, 2004,** ISBN-13: 978-1613082454

Professor Steve Peters

Another great book that influenced me was the *Chimp Paradox* by Professor Steve Peters. It's a modern take on explaining the *ego*, or *id*. It fits rather nicely into modern thinking, as opposed to the rather intense and traditional psychological theory of self and ego.

"The Chimp Paradox: The Acclaimed Mind Management Programme to Help You Achieve Success, Confidence and Happiness"
— **Prof. Steve Peters, 2012,** ISBN-13: 978-0091935580

Ben Hunt-Davies

Winning an Olympic medal and being the best there is in the world at the time is an awesome achievement. The book by Olympic Gold medallist Ben Hunt-Davies promotes the simple question *"Will it make the boat go faster?"* and is a great reminder about keeping focus on goals. If you don't get the book, visit the website and read-a-plenty (Search: *will it make the boat go faster*).

"Will it make the boat go faster?"
— **Ben Hunt-Davis, MBE and Harriet Beveridge, 2011,**
 ISBN-13: 978-1848769663

NHS Websites

Of the many websites I used in research, the **NHS Choices** site contained the most detailed, comprehensive and helpful material. For a Government website, it has been a joy to read through some of its many pages. It is succinct, wonderfully clear of jargon and has lots of multimedia applications that demonstrate various points. The *Live Well* section has lots of information on both physical health and mental wellbeing, with sections especially for students.

NHS Choices: www.nhs.uk
NHS Health A-Z: www.nhs.uk/Conditions
NHS Live Well: www.nhs.uk/Livewell
NHS Student Health: www.nhs.uk/Livewell/Studenthealth and www.nhs.uk/Livewell/Studenthealth/Pages/Mentalhealth.aspx

MAX YOUR DEGREE

Your Notes

THINK SMART. WORK SMART.

MAX YOUR DEGREE

www.ingramcontent.com/pod-product-compliance
Lightning Source LLC
Chambersburg PA
CBHW061652040426
42446CB00010B/1707